Contain It!

ENGLISH PAPER-PIECED STYLE ACCESSORIES

Linda
Chaney

American Quilter's Society
PO Box 3290 • Paducah, KY 42002-3290
Fax 270-898-1173 • email: orders@AQSquilt.com

Laura
Chaney Gerth

MW00337595

Located in Paducah, Kentucky, the American Quilter's Society (AQS) is dedicated to promoting the accomplishments of today's quilters. Through its publications and events, AQS strives to honor today's quiltmakers and their work and to inspire future creativity and innovation in quiltmaking.

EXECUTIVE BOOK EDITOR: ELAINE H. BRELSFORD
BOOK EDITOR: KATHY DAVIS
COPY EDITOR: CHRYSTAL ABHALTER
ILLUSTRATIONS: SARAH BOZONE, LYNDA SMITH
PROOFREADER: JOANN TREECE
GRAPHIC DESIGN: SARAH BOZONE
COVER DESIGN: MICHAEL BUCKINGHAM
QUILT PHOTOGRAPHY: CHARLES R. LYNCH

All rights reserved. No part of this book may be reproduced, stored in any retrieval system, or transmitted in any form, or by any means including but not limited to electronic, mechanical, photocopy, recording or otherwise, without the written consent of the author and publisher. Patterns may be copied for personal use only, including the right to enter contests; quilter should seek written permission from the author and pattern designer before entering. Credit must be given to the author, pattern designer, and publisher on the quilt label and contest entry form. Written permission from author, pattern designer, and publisher must be sought to raffle or auction quilts made from this book. While every effort has been made to ensure that the contents of this publication are as accurate and correct as possible, no warranty is provided nor results guaranteed. Since the author and AQS have no control over individual skills or choice of materials and tools, they do not assume responsibility for the use of this information.

Attention Photocopying Service: Please note the following— Publisher and author give permission to print pages 19, 21, 22, 25, 26, 28, 29, 32–34, 36–41, 43–46, 49–53, 56–63, 65–72, 75–79, 81–91, 94–99, 102–105, 109 for personal use only.

Additional copies of this book may be ordered from the American Quilter's Society, PO Box 3290, Paducah, KY 42002-3290, or online at www.AmericanQuilter.com.

Text and illustrations © 2014, Authors, Linda Chaney and Laura Chaney Gerth
Artwork © 2014, American Quilter's Society

American Quilter's Society
PO Box 3290 • Paducah, KY 42002-3290
Fax 270-898-1173 • email: orders@AQSquilt.com

Library of Congress Cataloging-in-Publication Data

Chaney, Linda.
   Contain it! : English paper-pieced style accessories / Linda Chaney and Laura Chaney Gerth.
      pages cm
   ISBN 978-1-60460-132-9
   1. Quilting–Patterns. 2. Patchwork–Patterns. 3. Containers.
   4. Vases. 5. Bowls (Tableware) I. Gerth, Laura Chaney. II. Title.
   TT835.C437 2014
   746.46–dc23
                                                2014008240

DEDICATION

To Grammy, who started and supported
our quilting journey.

To a Quilter

My quilting hands are never still
As long as I can see
But riding down the road at night
Became a chore to me.

My teacher, Barb, designed this hat
So I could sew a patch.
Though darkness is all around the car
I know my points will match.

The semi-drivers all go insane
As they look down on me.
Content and happy with needle in hand,
With a bright light so I can see.

So, Quilters, if you feel forlorn
And hate to waste a minute,
Just grab a hat and find a light
And put your head right in it.

Your husband may not see your way,
The neighbors may harass you.
But keep right on the quilting path,
Who knows—I just might pass you!!!

Mary Chaney
Montpelier Crazy Quilters

ACKNOWLEDGMENTS

Special thanks go to my husband, Bill, who has supported me throughout all phases of my quilting career, including the growth of my stash—does it ever stop? His constant encouragement during the writing of this book and his sense of humor kept me going. My son, Bill, was always a willing listener and would calmly try to help me solve my computer problems. I would also like to thank three friends—Christina Miller, Darlene McCord, and Kim Rothgeb—for their willingness to read the rough copies, give constructive criticism, and make containers.

Linda Chaney

This book wouldn't have been possible without Mom. She is the creative genius behind each of the containers and the methods of construction. I am merely her guinea pig and the occasional voice of clarity in writing patterns. I also want to thank my dad and my baby brother, Billy Chaney, who supported me during this crazy adventure. I couldn't have done this without Brandon Roseen who encouraged me every step of the way.

Laura Chaney Gerth

Together, we'd like to express our utmost thanks to our editor at the American Quilter's Society, Kathy Davis. Kathy has spent countless hours on the phone with us, answering our emails, and walking us through each step of this process. We also sincerely appreciate the support we've had from other staff members at AQS, including Elaine Brelsford, Meredith Schroeder, and Andi Reynolds.

Linda and Laura

CONTENTS

INTRODUCTION

A Bit of History

Welcome to the first book from Prairie Sewn Studios, a mother (Linda Chaney) and daughter (Laura Chaney Gerth) team who sew, quilt, shop, hoard fabric, create, scrapbook, frolic, eat, cry, enjoy, explore, learn, and write a book together!

In December 2005, I (Laura) was planning a May wedding. I went home to Omaha over the winter break, and as Mom and I were printing our homemade wedding invitations, I turned to her and said, "So, I had this idea...I should make quilts for my bridesmaids and soon-to-be in-laws." Mom, to her credit, didn't fall over but merely responded with, "Okay, let's go look at the stash and see what we can dig up." It was a crazy spring semester, but I did indeed finish a wallhanging for each bridesmaid and a full-sized quilt before the wedding. More importantly, Mom and I undertook our first ambitious sewing and quilting project together and came out alive on the other side. Mom also learned to fear the phrase "So, I had this idea..."

Three years later, it's Christmas 2008. My husband and I gave Mom a trip to the American Quilter's Society's Paducah Quilt Show as a Christmas present! I'd heard about the show from my grammy who used to travel to Kentucky every year with a group of her quilting girlfriends. Grammy was the person who got Mom and me hooked on quilting, so this trip not only meant a lot for our exploration of the art of quilting, but also for its personal connection and our memories of sewing with her.

Mom was beyond excited—looking forward to the show in April got us through a long challenging winter. That year became the first of this new mother-daughter annual tradition. Each year we see the show, take classes, meet quilting celebrities, buy lots of fabric, and get creative energy. In April 2011, our third annual trip, we signed up for a lecture and a demonstration on English paper piecing.

Mom didn't want to take the class; the English paper-piecing hexagon craze didn't especially interest her and I think she looked at the little pieces of paper with a bit of trepidation. I'd seen some of the nifty things people were doing with a modern take on Grandmother's Flower Garden and, because I'm her favorite (all right, only) daughter, Mom acquiesced. What do you know—it turns out Mom rather liked it! Paper pieces were bought and the basting fun began.

About six months later I was visiting Mom again and I turned to her and said the one phrase she'd learned to fear the most: "So I had this idea..." The next thing I knew I'd talked her into spending the rest of my visit designing a coaster using a single Grandmother's Flower Garden flower with Timtex™ for stabilizer. Afterwards, I continued making coasters while Mom's brain turned over an idea in her head, until one day she used Timtex as the foundation for a simple English paper-pieced style bowl!

This first version of the pattern and technique was refined again and again, and probably several more times, before she landed on the technique that we use today. She learned to draft patterns from vases and glassware so that the containers could be utilized for a wide variety of functions: live flowers, cocktail nuts, wrapped candies, and so on. I'd frequently get emails early in the morning telling me about how she woke up in the middle of the night with a new idea spinning around in her head and could not go back to sleep until she got up and sketched it out.

Mom joined an English paper-piecing sewing circle where she would work on her newest ideas each month. People started asking about her patterns and how they could learn to make them; my wheels started turning on how to transform Mom's work into a pattern line or book. When it was time to choose our classes for the 2012 AQS Paducah show, I went into the selection process with a secret agenda: talk to the AQS executive editor.

At each AQS quilt show, there are usually a few free lectures and presentations about what it takes to publish a book and how to submit a proposal to AQS. Again, Mom was hesitant (that's the polite way to say she thought I was absolutely nuts), but again, I'm her favorite daughter. So that April found us not only attending the publishing lecture, but also having an individual meeting with the executive editor herself. Much to Mom's surprise, the editor loved our idea and encouraged us to submit a proposal! After we took our samples back to the car and I picked Mom's jaw up off the floor, the fun began. We spent the entire seven-hour drive home talking about the project and hashing out a rough draft of the proposal.

After many hours of writing, working, and making revisions, we submitted the proposal. We didn't hear anything for a while and our confidence in the idea plummeted a bit more with each passing day. Then, the unexpected happened and Mom received a call from an administrator at AQS to tell us they wanted to publish our book! The contracts arrived in the mail a few days later and were signed and sent back. Only then did we realize how much work we had to do to actually write it.

The road to writing this book has been full of successes, failures, and possibly a bit of muttering under our breaths at our irons, needles, and fabric. We are so incredibly excited and humbled by this experience and can't believe that we have a book on the shelves, next to books by the various quilters we've admired for years. I know that if Grammy were still alive, she would be so proud of what we've done and tickled pink by the thought that her dedication to the quilting arts is what spurred us to undertake this journey.

The only possible downside to this whole process is that now, on more than one occasion, Mom has turned to me and with a mischievous twinkle in her eye said, "So, I have this idea…" and proceeds to tell me what our next book will be about!

Laura

For Whom Is This Book?

One of my favorite things about making containers is that I get to make design and sewing choices every time I sit down to plan one. What shape do I want to make? What size do I want? What foundation stabilizer should I use? Should I quilt the sides? Machine or hand sew? Fabric? Buttons? Trim? Beadwork?

These containers are also great because you can sew at any skill level and end up with a great completed project. If you're a beginner crafter, start with the basic shapes to build your confidence. The whipstitch is, in my opinion, the easiest hand stitch there is, even easier than the running stitch you usually link with hand sewing. Fusible tape will assure you have a good clean edge to sew and will keep everything snug and attached while you make the container. Advanced crafters can choose more challenging shapes, add detailed embellishments and quilting, and experiment with different fabric types.

The projects in this book are arranged from the simplest—a hexagon flatwork mug rug—to the most difficult—a star-shaped box. Start with an easy project in the beginning of the book before moving on to the harder ones at the end. Take your time and have fun blending your own creative ideas with those presented here. At the end of each project are additional template patterns to mix and match using the same instructions given for the main project. There are so many possible combinations of sides and bases, heights and widths, that you could make a hundred containers and none of them might be the same as another.

We find making these containers to be relaxing. If you enjoy having hand sewing to do while you watch TV—these are perfect projects. We both like to prepare several projects at once, keeping the pieces together in quart-size freezer bags. We then just grab the one we want to work on next, thread our needles, and get to work. We take them on road trips, plane rides, or work on them while just hanging out with friends.

Here are a few ideas for using the containers:
- Hostess gifts
- Teacher gifts
- Paper clip, pen, business card, and note pad holders
- Flower vases with glass inserts
- Candy, cocktail mint, or nut dishes
- TV remote, key, or coin bowls
- Thread catchers for a sewing machine
- Holiday and party table decorations

Obviously some containers work better than others if you intend to use them for a specific purpose, but don't be afraid to experiment. Some of our favorite designs have come from making a mistake somewhere! You, too, will also find your own creative ideas and uses for the containers you make.

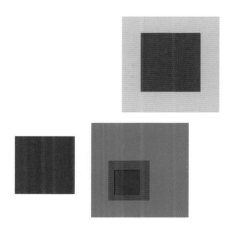

NUTS AND BOLTS

Basic Supplies

- Acrylic ruler
- Mechanical pencil
- Fabric marker
- Fine-tip permanent marker
- Heavy-duty template plastic (preferred) or heavy cardboard
- Scissors to cut the template plastic or cardboard
- Scissors to cut fabric
- 45mm rotary cutter
- 28mm rotary cutter
- Rotary-cutting mat
- ¼" Steam-A-Seam 2® Double Stick fusible web, Pellon® Lite EZ-Steam™ II Tape, or Stitch Witchery® by Dritz®
- Stabilizer: Buckram, Pellon® 70 Peltex® Sew-In Ultra Firm, or Timtex™ Interfacing
- Fusible lightweight interfacing, if embellishing
- Fabric
- Thread
- Needle
- Thimble
- Chopstick or orange stick for turning corners
- Clover® Wonder Clips (small) or flathead pins
- Steam iron
- Magnetic décor hook (optional)
- Velcro® Hook and Loop, Sew-On, or Fabric Fusion™ tape (optional)
- Embellishments—buttons, yarn, rickrack, gems, beads, as desired

Template Media

Heavy-duty template plastic works best for these projects and is sold in many general crafting or quilting stores. Regular template plastic can be used but will curl around the edges and is easily nicked by a rotary cutter. You may also use heavy cardboard to make templates. Take the time to create sturdy and accurate templates so that you can use them again and again.

Stabilizer

The choice of stabilizer is dependent upon the intended use and artist's choice for each project.

Buckram is a scrim fabric. When made from 100 percent cotton, it has a starch and resin finish that adds stiffness to a project, is dry cleanable only, and is commonly found in fabric stores. Buckram can also be made from woven or non-woven polyester which is both washable and dry cleanable and is most often found in drapery supply shops and online.

Pellon makes 70 Peltex Sew-In Ultra Firm Stabilizer, a 100 percent polyester material that is smooth and easy to cut in any direction. More rigid than buckram, it can be easily shaped with steam pressing. Available in white or black, it is washable and dry cleanable, and found at most sewing stores.

Timtex Interfacing is 100 percent polyester and is stiffer, firmer, and a bit heavier than Peltex but still easy to cut in any direction. It is washable and available in white.

These stabilizers are often found in 20"–22" widths in craft and sewing stores. For larger projects, wider widths of buckram and 70 Peltex can be found online.

Fabric

Any good quality cotton can be used, including scraps, pieced remnants, orphan blocks, or uncut yardage. Flannel, corduroy, upholstery fabric, speaker cloth, and indoor/outdoor fabric can also be used.

Keep in mind that the fabric will determine the washability of the container! If the fabric is not washable, the container will not be washable.

The type of fabric may dictate the container pattern used. Heavier materials, like upholstery or indoor/outdoor fabrics, are recommended only for projects constructed without sharp points.

Very little fabric is required to make the containers. Most of them can be created with less than ¼ yard of fabric. Charm squares, Layer Cakes™, fat eighths, fat quarters, and scraps work well for making these containers.

Basting Material

Using ¼" double-sided fusible tape that can be repositioned before ironing in place is preferable to hand basting when joining the fabric to stabilizer. The fusible tape maintains the integrity of each component of a container and holds the stabilizer in position when the project is turned right-side out upon completion. In addition, there are no basting stitches to be removed, especially from tight corners.

Steam-A-Seam 2, Lite EZ-Steam II, and Stitch Witchery are sold in ¼" x 20 yard rolls. Several projects can be made from each package.

A word of caution: we do not recommend using a dryer, any type of fabric softener, or dryer sheets for cleaning containers assembled with fusible tape, as is indicated on the fusible tape packaging.

Fusible Interfacing

Embellishing by machine or by hand will be enhanced if interfacing is fused to the wrong side of the fabric to be embellished. The interfacing will stabilize the fabric, preventing distortion and stretching. Several brands are currently available. Experiment with a few to find your favorite.

Needles, Thread, Clips, and Pins

Any good quality thread and needle will work. If one combination does not sew smoothly, try changing the type of thread or needle. Size 7 betweens needles and Mettler® Metrosene Plus thread are a good combination for sewing Peltex and Timtex pieces together. A thinner needle, such as a size 11 Richard Hemming & Son™ large-eye milliners needle, used with Mettler Metrosene Plus thread works best for sewing buckram together. A thimble will help eliminate sore fingers!

Consider the thread color. Matching the thread to the fabric will hide many stitching flaws; however, there may be times when you want the stitches to show as part of the overall design. Machine stitching with invisible thread can be quite useful and the project may go together faster. Be sure to use good quality thread.

To help hold seams together while sewing, flathead pins can be used but small Clover Wonder Clips may be preferable. They are easy to use and won't distort the thick layers while sewing.

Embellishments

Numerous techniques can be used to embellish any project. It really depends on your imagination and willingness to play. Beads, buttons, ribbons, yarns, trims, and threads can be used for embellishing, including the different decorative stitches on your sewing machine. Be sure to apply a lightweight fusible interfacing on the wrong side of the fabric before embellishing.

Whatever embellishment you plan to use, consider the final function of the container. Is it purely decorative? Is it functional? Does it need to be laundered occasionally? Is it for a child? Will the embellishments be compatible with the fabric?

Glass or Plastic Inserts

After a project is completed, you may wish to insert a glass or plastic bottle, bowl, vase, or cube. The insert will not only provide additional support but will protect the inside of the project from flowers, paper clips, cotton swabs, nuts, or candies. The insert doesn't need to be fancy or expensive since with most completed containers, it won't be seen. Check out your favorite bargain store!

A Gallery of Inserts

Hand Sewing Techniques

Knowledge of several hand-sewing techniques will be beneficial to the construction of any project. The whipstitch and ladder stitches are used on most projects.

Quilter's Knot
A quilter's knot is a quick method to knot the end of the thread. Directions are given for right-handers; left-handers should use the opposite hand.

Step 1: Hold the threaded needle in your left hand with the eye of needle to the left.

Step 2: Bring the long tail of the thread up and lay it along the needle with the tail pointing toward the eye of the needle.

Step 3: Hold the tail of the thread on the needle with the thumb and forefinger of your left hand. Wrap the thread around the needle with your right hand 3–5 times. The more times you wrap the thread, the larger the knot.

Step 4: Pinch the wrapped threads around the needle with your left hand and pull the needle to the right through the coiled threads with your right hand. The knot will slide off the eye and down the threads.

Step 5: While holding the knot, pull the needle until the knot is at the long end of the thread.

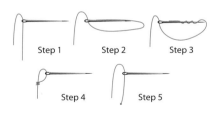

Step 1   Step 2   Step 3

Step 4   Step 5

Quilter's Knot

Running Stitch
The running stitch consists of a single line of straight stitches. When the thread is pulled, the fabric can be gathered along the edge. Use longer stitches and gently pull to prevent the thread from breaking.

Running Stitch

Whipstitch
The whipstitch is used to join fabrics along a seam with either right or wrong sides together. The stitches are about 1/16"–1/8" apart and only deep enough to catch a few threads of fabric. Instructions are given for right-handers to work from the right to the left; left-handers work from the left to the right.

Thread the needle with matching thread and use a quilter's knot on one end. Place two pieces of fabric together. Holding them in one hand, insert the needle at the beginning of the seam line into the back of the fabrics, and catch one or two threads of both pieces of fabric. Pull the needle toward you through the fabrics. The needle and the stitch will be perpendicular to the edge of the fabric.

Return the needle to the back of the fabrics and again insert the needle into the back about 1/16"–1/8" distance from the first stitch. Take a small bite of fabric and pull the needle through both fabric pieces toward you.

Continue to whipstitch the length of the seam. Tie off with a knot of your choice.

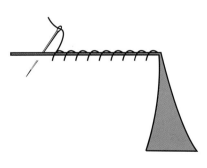

Whipstitch

Ladder Stitch
The ladder stitch is also used to join two edges together. When the thread is tightened, the stitches should be virtually invisible. Right-handers work the stitch from the right to the left. Left-handers will work from the left to the right.

The thread is buried in the inside edge of the first fabric. Take small stitches, following the red arrows, as the needle and thread go from the edge of the first fabric to the edge of the second fabric. Horizontal arrows represent a stitch that is buried in the fabric along the edge. Vertical arrows represent stitches crossing from one fabric edge to the other.

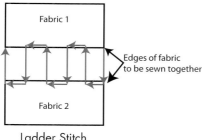

Ladder Stitch

General Directions

The following directions will be used in all of the projects in this book and should be read carefully before starting any project. They provide detailed step-by-step instructions required to complete each container successfully. Additional comments and tips for each container can be found within each set of specific instructions. The projects have been arranged from the simplest to the most complicated.

LESSONS FROM LAURA

Start with the flatwork project to practice applying fusible tape to fuse the fabric onto the stabilizer before beginning your first three-dimensional project. Then, master the basics of the whole technique by making a cube before making some of the more unusual shapes.

- Choose a stabilizer—buckram, Peltex, or Timtex.

- Select the fabric. Fussy cutting specific design motifs from the fabric will require more fabric. Create your own fabrics by sewing bits and pieces together for a scrappy look. Select one fabric to complete the entire project or choose different fabrics for various parts of the project.

A fussy-cut scalloped bowl

Make the Templates

From each pattern for your chosen project, trace one stabilizer template and one fabric template onto template material.

- To create a stabilizer template, trace the inner solid line. Accuracy is critical since this template will be used to make the "bones" of the project.

- To create a fabric template, trace the outer dotted line from the pattern. This creates a template that is ½" larger on all sides than the stabilizer template. To feature a specific fussy-cut design motif on the container, trace the solid stabilizer line onto the fabric template to create a design window for viewing what part of the fabric will be seen on the finished project.

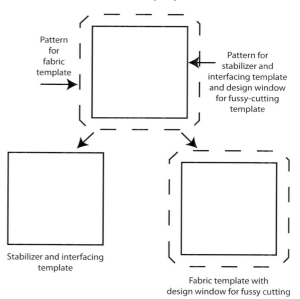

Create a fabric and a stabilizer template from each project template.

- The three-dimensional containers use:
    - Inner side and inner base fabric templates
    - Inner side and inner base stabilizer and interfacing templates
    - Outer side and outer base fabric templates
    - Outer side and outer base stabilizer and interfacing templates

- Label each template using a permanent marker with:
    - The name of the container project
    - The type of template: Fabric or Stabilizer and Interfacing

♦ Outer or Inner
♦ Side or Base
♦ Marks of significant direction (center, bottom, top, arrow)
♦ Snip marks on concave containers

• Cut out each template carefully trimming just inside the outer line to remove it.

• Check the accuracy of the templates by placing them on top of the pattern. If discrepancies are noticeable, remake the template.

LESSONS FROM LAURA

A great way to store the templates for each project is to put them in a quart-size freezer bag. Label the bag, punch a hole in the top corner, and collect the bags on a book ring. Having spent time making the templates, you don't want to lose them!

Cut the Stabilizer Pieces

• Lightly trace the stabilizer template onto the stabilizer with a fine-point permanent marker. Transfer all of the information on the template onto the stabilizer piece.

• Cut out the stabilizer with scissors or a rotary cutter.

LESSONS FROM LAURA

When using a rotary cutter to cut the stabilizer, place a piece of stabilizer under the unsupported edge of the ruler to increase its stability.

• Dry fit the inner stabilizer pieces to be sure they are cut accurately. Place the inner side stabilizer pieces around the inner base stabilizer. The bottom edges of the inner side stabilizer pieces should be the same length as the edges of the inner base stabilizer. The same is true for the outer sides and outer bases. If they are not the same, check the templates and recut them correctly.

LESSONS FROM LAURA

Accuracy is really important. Being off by even ⅛" can have a rippling effect on the entire project. Dry fitting saves you from the frustration of basting all of the fabric onto the stabilizer and then sewing the pieces together before discovering a template accuracy issue. Trust me—this is no fun.

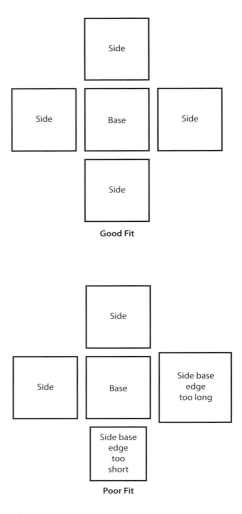

Dry fit to ensure that the edges match in length.

Cut the Fabric Pieces

• Iron any creases and wrinkles from the fabric before marking and cutting it.

• Multiple fabric pieces can be cut at one time from a stack of fabrics or you may wish to fussy cut them individually to create design motifs.

• Trace the inner side and inner base fabric templates and the outer side and outer base fabric templates onto the fabric. If fussing cutting motifs, center the design window drawn on the template over the area of the fabric that you wish to appear on the container.

• If heavy template plastic is used to create the fabric template, use a 28mm rotary cutter to cut

Chaney and Gerth ▪▪▪ Contain It!

the fabric. Otherwise, trace the template and then carefully cut the fabric with scissors.

- Lightly label the fabric pieces on the wrong side of the fabric, if necessary, using a fabric-safe pencil or chalk marker.

Cut and Fuse the Interfacing

If you plan to embellish a fabric piece by machine or hand, fusing lightweight interfacing to the wrong side of the fabric will add stability and help prevent stretching.

- Using the stabilizer template, trace and cut out the interfacing.

- Center the interfacing on the wrong side of the fabric, making sure the adhesive side of the interfacing faces the wrong side of the fabric.

- Fuse into place following the manufacturer's directions.

- Transfer any necessary labels marked on the fabric to the interfacing.

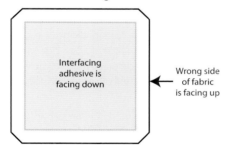

Fuse the interfacing to the wrong side of the fabric.

Fuse the Fabric and Stabilizer Pieces Together

- Pair the fabric inner sides and fabric inner bases with the corresponding stabilizer inner sides and stabilizer inner bases, making sure that any arrows on a pair of pieces point in the same direction.

- Pair the fabric outer sides and fabric outer bases to the corresponding stabilizer outer sides and stabilizer outer bases, making sure that any arrows on a pair of pieces point in the same direction.

- Fuse one pair together at a time.

LESSONS FROM LAURA

An old piece of cotton fabric placed on an ironing board before applying the fusible tape to the stabilizer pieces will prevent the accidental gumming of the ironing board. It's far easier to dispose of a small piece of fabric than the entire ironing board cover!

- Place a fabric piece on the ironing board wrong-side up. Run the iron over it for just a second to heat the fabric to make applying the fusible tape easier.

- Center the corresponding stabilizer on the fabric. Ensure that the fabric edges are equally exposed by ½" around all edges of the stabilizer.
  - ♦ If centering a fussy-cut fabric design, carefully pick up the fabric and stabilizer and check the right side of the fabric for correct design placement.

  - ♦ Any markings on the stabilizer should be visible and facing up.

  - ♦ The stabilizer should match and cover any fused interfacing ironed to the fabric.

- Place the ¼" fusible tape carefully along the one edge of the stabilizer. Be sure the fusible tape does not extend past the outer edges of the stabilizer since these edges will be stitched.

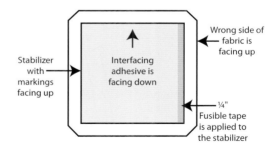

Place the fusible tape along the edges of the stabilizer.

- Apply the fusible tape to the stabilizer in the following order to reduce bulk:
  - ♦ On the outer sides, fuse the left and right edges first and then the top and bottom.

  - ♦ On the inner sides, fuse the top and bottom first and then the left and right edges.

  - ♦ On the outer and inner bases, fuse the tape in

a clockwise or counterclockwise direction. Be consistent in the direction you have chosen.

♦ On the flatwork pieces, fuse the tape in a clockwise or counterclockwise direction.

LESSONS FROM LAURA

When applying fusible tape, a small travel iron is much lighter and more convenient to use than a large iron. It is also easier to see the fusing process, resulting in fewer burned fingers.

- Fold the fabric edges carefully over the edge of the stabilizer and cover the fusible tape. Iron with steam for 2–3 seconds. Ensure that the folded fabric completely covers the fusible tape to prevent the gumming of the iron.

- Be sure the fabric is snug along the edge of the stabilizer.

- Continue fusing the fabric to the stabilizer until all of the edges are covered.

- If the fused fabric seems bulky, trim the excess fabric.

- Curved edges require additional steps.

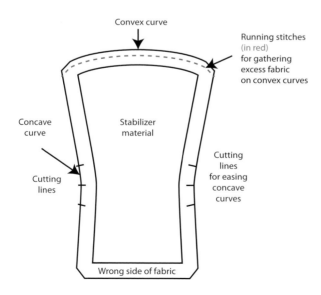

Concave and convex edge treatments

A concave vase (left) and a convex vase (right)

- ♦ For concave sides, small slits must be snipped into the fabric along the curved edge. Make several ¼" slits about ½" apart to help ease the fusing process. Do not snip all the way to the stabilizer.

- ♦ For convex sides, the fabric must be slightly gathered and fused along the curved edge. This can be accomplished in one of two ways:
  ❖ Gather lightly by hand and press, or

  ❖ Sew a running stitch about ⅛" from the edge of the fabric. Gently pull the thread to gather the fabric along the curved edges after the fusible tape has been placed along the edge; press. Remove the thread after fusing with the fusible tape.

- After fusing, turn the piece over and press right-side up for several seconds.

- Fuse all of the inner side, outer side, inner base, and outer base pieces for the project.

LESSONS FROM LAURA

If you discover you have fused incorrectly, you can remove the fused fabric from the stabilizer. Iron with steam over the piece for a few seconds to heat the fusible tape and carefully pull the fabric and the stabilizer apart.

Quilt or Embellish

- Unless indicated otherwise in the directions for a specific project, quilt or embellish the sides and bases of the container, if desired.

- Decorative machine or hand stitches, different threads and yarns, beadwork, or buttons can enhance the beauty of the container. If adding a magnet, determine which side or base will hold the magnet. Do not embellish the side or base where the magnet will be used.

- Sign the outer base with a permanent, fabric-safe pen. Include any personal messages or information about the container, including the date and your name.

Assemble the *Octopus*

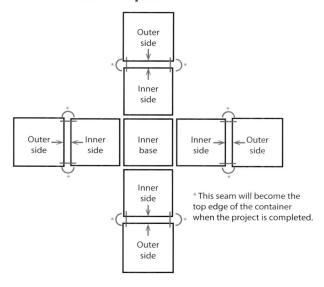

Arrange the octopus.

*This seam will become the top edge of the container when the project is completed.

- The *octopus* is the configuration of connected sides and bases of each project. You may connect the pieces by hand or machine.

- Each container project will have its own unique octopus shape.

- Arrange the fused fabric and stabilizer pieces on a flat surface right-side up as they will be sewn. Be sure the arrows on the side pieces are pointing toward the seam that will become the top edge of the container when the project is completed. Center the slightly smaller inner side pieces along the slightly larger outer side pieces.

Methods for Sewing the Octopus

LESSONS FROM LAURA

You may choose to sew most seams by machine or by hand. Machine stitching works best on straight edges. Hand stitching works best on curves. If embellishments are to be added to the edges of the pieces, it may be preferable to join the seams by hand.

Machine-Stitched Method

- Select the thread color carefully as the zigzag stitch will be visible along the top edge of the finished project.

- Align the edges of the two pieces to be sewn together, side by side and right-side up. When sewing a smaller inner side to a larger outer side, center the inner side along the outer side.

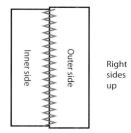

Center the inner side along the outer side.

- Push the edges of the two pieces together so no gap is present. Using a very narrow and short zigzag stitch, sew them together. Be certain that both pieces of fabric are caught by the stitches but avoid catching the stabilizer.

- After stitching, check the seam for gaps or holes. Holding the sewn seam up to a light illuminates these openings. This is especially important if the top edges of the container are machine stitched since the gaps will be visible on the finished container. Repair if necessary.

- Repeat for all of the remaining inner side and outer side pairs.

- Attach an inner side to the inner base using the same technique as above. The right sides will be facing up on the sewing machine.

- Attach the remaining inner side pieces to the inner base and look for gaps or holes in the seams.

- The project will now look like an octopus.

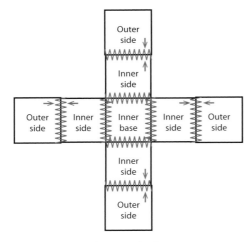

A machine-stitched octopus

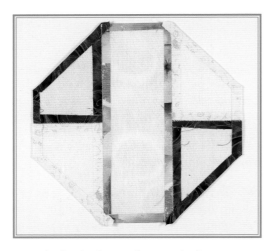

The back of a machine-stitched piece

Hand-Sewn Method

- Some embellishments, such as ribbon, rickrack, or beaded ribbon, can be added to the top edge or side seams as the inner and outer seams are joined.

- Select the thread color carefully since the stitches may show.

- Tie a knot in the thread and, using a whipstitch, stitch two paired pieces with right sides together along the top edge. End with a knot.

- Reinforce the first and last stitches by making two knots or by taking a backstitch.

- Repeat for all of the remaining inner side and outer side pairs.

> **LESSONS FROM LAURA**
>
> Pull each stitch snugly; you don't want holes in the seams! Do not be afraid of breaking the thread. If, or really when, the thread breaks, simply tie a new knot, go back a few stitches to sew over several previous stitches, and continue stitching past the thread break. This will keep the seam firmly together.

- With the right sides together, whipstitch the bottom edge of an inner side piece to one edge of the inner base.

- Attach the remaining inner side pieces to the inner base.

- The project will now look like an octopus.

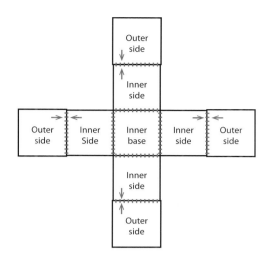

A hand-sewn octopus

Add a Magnet

Magnetic décor hooks

- You may wish to include a magnet in your container so it can be used on a refrigerator or other metal surface. Be sure to use a magnetic décor hook found in hardware stores. Craft magnets are not strong enough to support the weight of a container and its contents.

- Before hand sewing the long side seams of the octopus together, attach hook and loop pieces of Velcro about ⅔ of the width of the edge to create a pocket to hold the magnet in place.

- The Velcro pieces are attached to the stabilizer of an inner side and an outer side or an inner base and an outer base.

- Use the diagram below to make sure the Velcro is attached in the correct place. If in doubt, insert pins in the Velcro locations and fold the octopus to see if the Velcro pieces match up correctly. When correctly placed and the inner and outer pieces are folded together, the Velcro will adhere to itself creating a pocket which can be opened to insert a magnet.

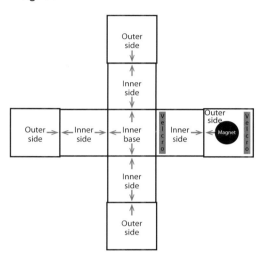

The placement of the Velcro and a magnet is shown from the back side of an octopus.

- Following the manufacturer's directions, sew or fuse the Velcro hook and loop tapes into place.

- When attaching the outer base to the outer side pieces, do not stitch the edge where the Velcro is attached and where the magnet will be inserted. Instead, attach the outer base to the inner base.

- Insert the magnet into the pocket. If the magnet has a hook, just pound it down so it lies flat against the magnet. Be sure to position the magnetic side of the magnet to face outward so it can connect with the metal surface from which it will hang.

- Firmly press the Velcro hook and loop sections together to hold the magnet in place.

- Remove the magnet before laundering the container.

Container Completion

• The remainder of the container assembly is hand sewn.

• With the right sides together, match the top and bottom edges of one long side to the side next to it.

> **LESSONS FROM LAURA**
>
> I use a pin at the seam between the inner and outer pieces to hold it together when I'm sewing. Carefully match the sides together and sew securely or you'll end up with a hole on the top edge of your container!

• Whipstitch the entire length of the seam between the two long sides beginning with a reinforcing backstitch or knot at the junction of the inner base and the inner sides. Don't be afraid to fold the inner base a bit to help sew a tight corner.

• In sewing the long side seam, make 2–3 stitches on the lip formed by the junction of the outer and inner side pieces. This lip is caused by the outer side being slightly larger than the inner side and is necessary to allow the outer side to fold into place when the container is finished.

• Whipstitch to the end of the long side seam and finish it with a reinforcing backstitch or knot.

• Match and whipstitch the remaining long sides together until the container shape is complete.

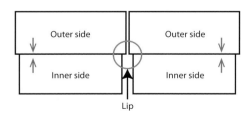

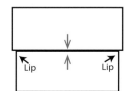

Formation of a lip

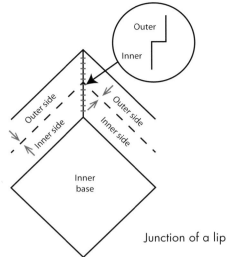

Junction of a lip

• Turn the container right-side out by folding the outer sides down over the inner sides.

• Be sure all of the corners and seams are fully turned and aligned. Push out each corner completely with a chopstick or orange stick.

• Turn the container upside down and lay the outer base on top of the inner base with wrong sides together.

• Align one edge of the outer base with one edge of an outer side. Use a ladder stitch or whipstitch to attach the outer base to each outer side edge.

• Backstitch to reinforce the outer base stitches at each corner.

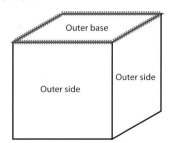

The outer base is whipstitched to the outer sides.

• Knot and bury thread.

• Press the top edges of the container, if needed. Add embellishments, if desired.

• Enjoy the completed container.

PROJECTS

Flatwork Practice Projects

Not sure about trying your hand at a container just yet? Try a flatwork practice project first. The same techniques used to construct the containers will create a flatwork project. The only difference—no side seams, just a base. A small flatwork project might be a coaster; a larger one might be a placemat. You can even make a table topper. The size and shape is all up to you! Use any of the template patterns in this book or draw your own to make flatwork pieces tailor-made for anywhere in your home or office.

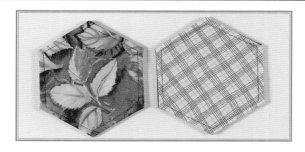

Hexagon Mug Rug

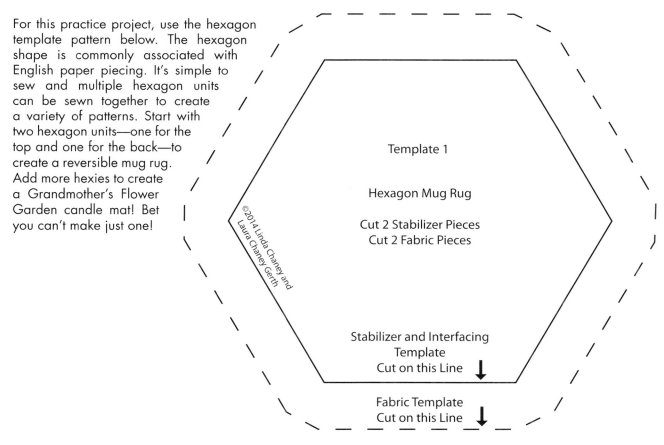

For this practice project, use the hexagon template pattern below. The hexagon shape is commonly associated with English paper piecing. It's simple to sew and multiple hexagon units can be sewn together to create a variety of patterns. Start with two hexagon units—one for the top and one for the back—to create a reversible mug rug. Add more hexies to create a Grandmother's Flower Garden candle mat! Bet you can't make just one!

Materials

(2) 5" x 5" fabric squares or scraps. The top and back can be different fabrics.

Stabilizer—3½" x 8"

¼" fusible tape

Template material

Lightweight fusible interfacing (optional)

Assembly

The construction steps are summarized below, but refer to the general directions on pages 9–16 for more detail.

- Using Template 1, trace the stabilizer and fabric template patterns onto template material and then cut them out.

- Label the templates with the information printed on the template pattern.

Template 1

Hexagon Mug Rug

Cut 2 Stabilizer Pieces
Cut 2 Fabric Pieces

©2014 Linda Chaney and
Laura Chaney Gerth

Stabilizer and Interfacing
Template
Cut on this Line ↓

Fabric Template
Cut on this Line ↓

- Using the fabric template, cut 2 fabric pieces. Using the stabilizer template, cut 2 stabilizer pieces.

- If embellishing the fabric hexagons, use the stabilizer template to cut a lightweight fusible interfacing piece and apply it to the wrong side of the fabric to be embellished.

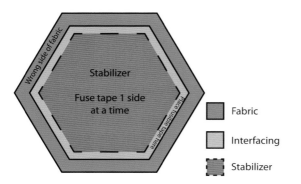

- Center the stabilizer hexagons on the wrong side of the fabrics, leaving ½" of fabric uncovered on all sides.

- Apply ¼" fusible tape to one edge of a stabilizer hexagon. Refer to page 11 for the order in which to apply the tape.

- Fold the fabric edge over the fusible tape on the stabilizer and fuse it to the tape one side at a time. Make sure that the folded fabric completely covers the fusible tape to prevent the gumming of the iron. Be careful not to stretch the bias-cut edges.

- Repeat the 2 steps above until all of the edges are covered with fabric.

- Quilt the hexagons with decorative stitches, if desired. Embellishments such as rickrack or cording can be added to the outside edges using fusible tape to attach it between the top and back pieces.

- Join the 2 hexagons, with the stabilizer sides together, using a machine zigzag stitch or whipstitching by hand around the outside edges.

- Press with an iron and enjoy your mug rug.

Pentagonal Star Mat

Assembly

The construction steps are summarized below, but refer to the assembly instructions for the Hexagon Rug Mug or the general directions on pages 9–16 for more detail.

- Using Template 2, prepare a fabric and a stabilizer template and label them. Cut 10 fabric pieces and 10 stabilizer pieces. Fuse the fabric and the stabilizer pieces together to make 10 diamonds. With the arrows on the templates pointing toward the center, sew 5 diamonds together for the top of the mat and 5 diamonds together for the back as shown in the diagram of a pentagonal star. Sew the edges of the 2 stars with wrong sides together.

- This would be great as a mobile, an ornament, or a candle mat. To hang it, place a loop of fabric or trim between the top and back stars at the point of a diamond before sewing the stars together.

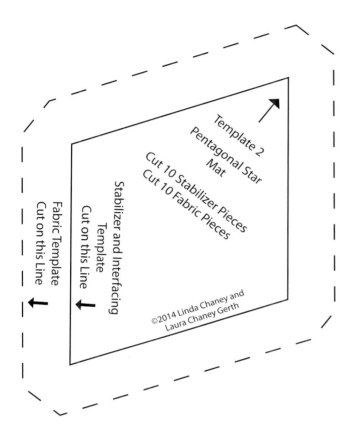

Template 2
Pentagonal Star
Mat
Cut 10 Stabilizer Pieces
Cut 10 Fabric Pieces

Stabilizer and Interfacing
Template
Cut on this Line

Fabric Template
Cut on this Line

©2014 Linda Chaney and
Laura Chaney Gerth

Wave Mat

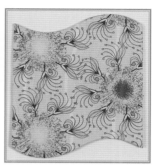

Assembly

The construction steps are summarized below, but refer to the assembly instructions for the Hexagon Rug Mug on pages 19–20 or the general directions on pages 9–16 for more detail.

- Template 3, the single wave template, can be used to make 1 or more waves in a mat. Each wave needs a top and a back. Determine the number of waves needed for the project and, using the single wave template, cut a fabric piece and a stabilizer piece to make the top of each wave in the mat. Turn the template over and cut a fabric piece and a stabilizer piece in reverse for the back of each wave. Be sure to label the pieces as either top or back to avoid confusion.

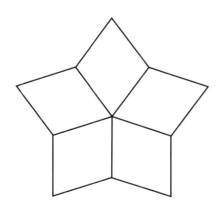

Diagram of a pentagonal star

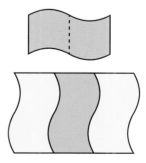

Designs made with the single wave template

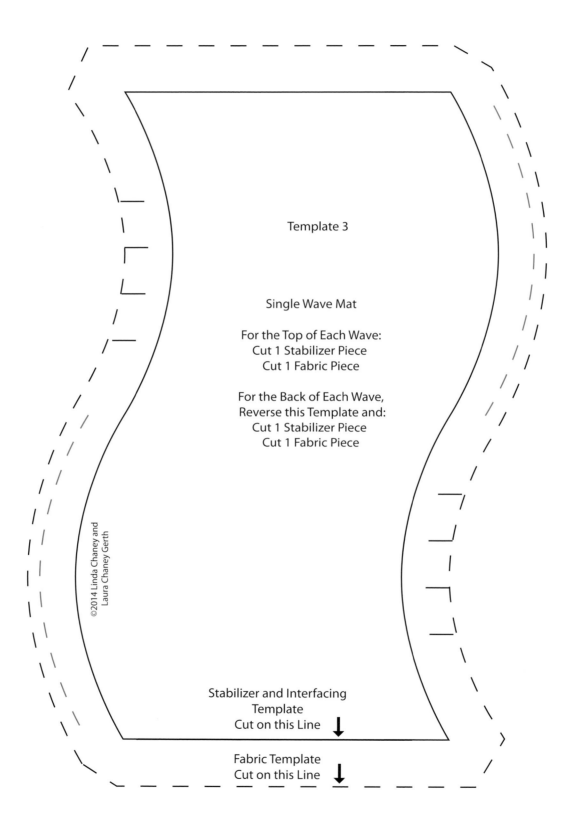

Template 3

Single Wave Mat

For the Top of Each Wave:
Cut 1 Stabilizer Piece
Cut 1 Fabric Piece

For the Back of Each Wave,
Reverse this Template and:
Cut 1 Stabilizer Piece
Cut 1 Fabric Piece

©2014 Linda Chaney and
Laura Chaney Gerth

Stabilizer and Interfacing
Template
Cut on this Line ↓

Fabric Template
Cut on this Line ↓

- Fuse a top fabric and a top stabilizer piece together to make the top of a wave mat. Using the reversed fabric and stabilizer pieces, make a second wave for the back of the mat. Place the 2 waves wrong sides together and sew around the outer edges.

- If you wish to make a multiple-wave mat with a single fabric as shown in the photo at the top of page 21, lay the single wave stabilizer and interfacing template on a sheet of paper and trace it. Move the template into the position for the second wave, aligning the side edges, and trace it again. Continue tracing waves until you have created a new template the size you wish. This will be the new stabilizer and interfacing template for the top of the project. Add a ½" border around the stabilizer and interfacing template to create a fabric template for the top. Then cut 1 top fabric piece and 1 top stabilizer piece with the two new templates.

- If using the new multiple-wave templates for the back of the mat, turn the templates over and cut 1 fabric piece and 1 stabilizer piece in reverse. Be sure to label the pieces as either top or back to avoid confusion.

- The single wave template can be cut in half to make 2 coasters. Multiple waves can be sewn together to make placemats or table runners. You can even make a flag. It's all up to you!

A Flatwork Gallery

The Cube Container

Cube, square, and rectangular containers are versatile, can be made in a variety of sizes and shapes, and are perfect additions on desks, counters, and tables. They can decorate and organize any room of your home or office while delighting everyone who sees them.

Cubes

We love the cube. It's cute, functional, and easy to put together. You can add a magnetic décor hook to the cube so it can be hung on a refrigerator or the metal wall of a cubicle or desk in an office. If you want to use a glass insert, check your local dollar store. A 3½" x 3½" x 3⅜" glass insert should easily fit inside the completed cube container.

Materials

(10) 5" x 5" charm squares, scraps, or 1 fat quarter

Stabilizer—15" x 20"

¼" fusible tape

Template material

Lightweight fusible interfacing (optional)

Magnetic décor hook, flat (optional)

¾" x 6" Velcro, fusible or sew-in (optional)

Assembly

The construction steps are summarized below, but refer to the general directions for more detail.

- Using Template 4 and Template 5, trace the stabilizer and fabric template patterns for the inner sides and inner base onto template material. Repeat using the template patterns for the outer base and outer sides.

- Label the templates with the information printed on the template pattern and cut them out.

LESSONS FROM LAURA

The cube is a great design to use with 5" charm squares—only 10 squares are needed—and gives you another reason to build a charm square stash! Mix and match the sides and bases with coordinating or contrasting colors.

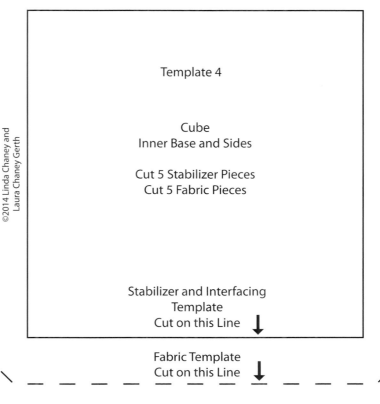

©2014 Linda Chaney and Laura Chaney Gerth

Template 4

Cube
Inner Base and Sides

Cut 5 Stabilizer Pieces
Cut 5 Fabric Pieces

Stabilizer and Interfacing
Template
Cut on this Line ↓

Fabric Template
Cut on this Line ↓

©2014 Linda Chaney and
Laura Chaney Gerth

Template 5

Cube
Outer Base and Sides

Cut 5 Stabilizer Pieces
Cut 5 Fabric Pieces

Stabilizer and Interfacing
Template
Cut on this Line ↓

Fabric Template
Cut on this Line ↓

• If embellishing the cube with embroidery, beads, or buttons, use the outer stabilizer template to cut a piece of interfacing for each outer side you want to embellish. Center the interfacing fusible-side down on the wrong side of the fabric, leaving ½" of fabric uncovered on all sides and then fuse.

Construction
• Pair the inner and outer fabrics with the inner and outer stabilizers. Work with one unit at a time.

• Center a stabilizer square on the wrong side of a fabric piece and leave ½" of fabric uncovered on all sides.

• Apply ¼" fusible tape to one edge of a stabilizer square. Refer to page 11 for the order in which to apply the tape.

LESSONS FROM LAURA

I like using my lazy susan-mounted rotary-cutting mat to cut the fabric for a cube. I stack the charm squares, place a template on them, and turn the cutting mat as I trim each side of the pieces.

Cutting
• Using the inner fabric template, cut 5 fabric squares.

• Using the outer fabric template, cut 5 fabric squares.

• Using the inner stabilizer template, cut 5 stabilizer squares.

• Using the outer stabilizer template, cut 5 stabilizer squares.

- Make sure that the folded fabric completely covers the fusible tape to prevent the gumming of the iron.

- Fold the fabric edge over the fusible tape and the stabilizer and fuse it to the tape one edge at a time.

- Repeat the 4 steps above until all of the stabilizer and fabric units are fused.

- Quilt the squares with decorative stitches, if desired.

- If adding a magnet, determine which side or base will hold the magnet. Attach hook and loop pieces of Velcro to create a pocket to hold the magnet in place. If adding embellishments, do not embellish the side where the magnet will be used. For additional details, see page 15.

- Lay out the octopus with right-sides up. For additional information on octopi, please see pages 13–15.

- Center an inner side top along an outer side top. The arrows on both pieces should point toward each other. Sew the inner side and the outer side together by machine or hand. Repeat to sew the remainder of the inner sides and outer sides together. Return the sides to their positions in the octopus. Machine and hand sewing methods are discussed on pages 13–16.

- Sew an inner side to one side of the inner base. Repeat to sew the remainder of the inner sides to the inner base.

- Sew the long side seams by hand. Refer to page 16 for information on sewing the lip created by the joining of the outer sides and the inner sides.

- Turn the container right-side out by folding the outer sides down over the inner sides with wrong sides together. Be sure all the corners and seams are fully turned and aligned.

- Turn the container upside down and lay the outer base on top of the inner base with wrong sides together.

- Align one edge of the outer base with one edge of an outer side. Use a ladder stitch or whipstitch to attach the outer base to each outer side edge, except the magnet pocket side, if a magnet is planned for the container. For the magnet pocket side, whipstitch the outer base to the inner base.

- Backstitch to reinforce the outer base stitches at each corner. Knot and bury thread.

- Press the top edges of the container, if needed. Add embellishments, if desired, and enjoy your new cube!

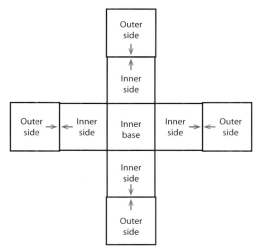

The Cube octopus

Squares and Rectangles

Assembly

- Using Templates 6–9 and the instructions for assembling a cube, create other square and rectangular containers including a mini cube. The Cube Base and Side templates on pages 25–26 can be mixed and matched with the templates below to make a small mini cube and short or tall rectangular containers.

- These containers will need 4 inner sides, 4 outer sides, 1 inner base, and 1 outer base. Just choose the templates you wish to use for the sides and the base and cut the number of pieces needed accordingly. Have fun!

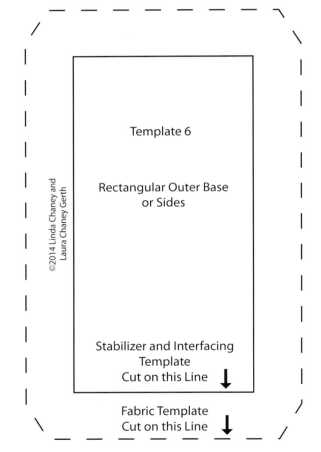

©2014 Linda Chaney and Laura Chaney Gerth

Template 6

Rectangular Outer Base or Sides

Stabilizer and Interfacing Template
Cut on this Line ↓

Fabric Template
Cut on this Line ↓

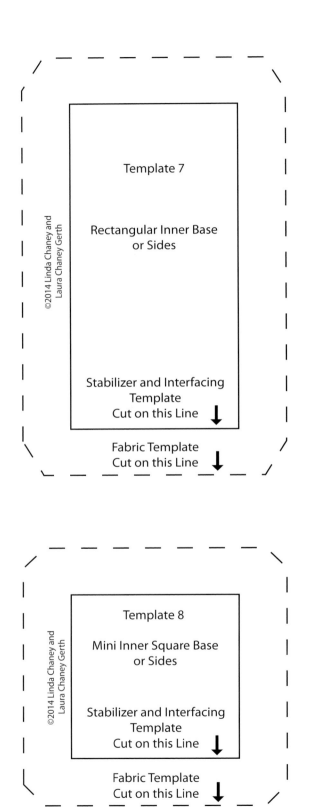

©2014 Linda Chaney and Laura Chaney Gerth

Template 7

Rectangular Inner Base or Sides

Stabilizer and Interfacing Template
Cut on this Line ↓

Fabric Template
Cut on this Line ↓

©2014 Linda Chaney and Laura Chaney Gerth

Template 8

Mini Inner Square Base or Sides

Stabilizer and Interfacing Template
Cut on this Line ↓

Fabric Template
Cut on this Line ↓

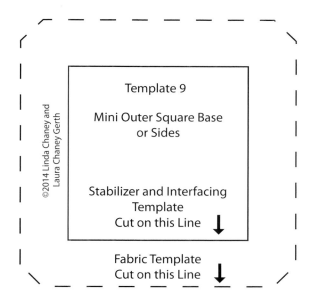

A Gallery of Cube and Rectangle Projects

Below are some octopi for containers you can make from the square and rectangular templates.

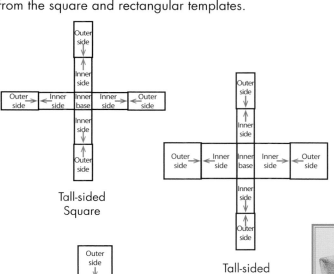

Tall-sided Square

Tall-sided Rectangle

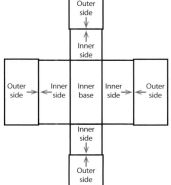

Short-sided Rectangle

The Concave Container

Concave bowls and vases have sides which curve inward. They provide a lot of flexibility for making creative containers. Dress one up or dress it down. It's all up to you, your imagination, and your decorating style.

LESSONS FROM LAURA

Don't limit yourself to using fabric containers for dry goods only. A glass container, bowl, or vase can be inserted into a container to hold fresh flowers. Check your local dollar store or thrift shop for inexpensive glass pieces.

Tall Flared Tulip Vase

This project is a concave flared vase with a square base. An old-fashioned flared soft drink glass inserted inside makes this container a truly unique vase. Choose one fabric for the outside and one for the inside or give the vase a scrappy look by using a variety of fabrics. Fussy cut the sides or add beaded trims to make it your own.

Materials

2 fat quarters—one for the inside and one for the outside or mix and match scraps

Stabilizer—20" x 20"

¼" fusible tape

Lightweight fusible interfacing (optional)

Assembly

The construction steps are summarized below, but refer to the general directions for more detail.

- Using Templates 10–13, trace the stabilizer and fabric template patterns for the inner sides and inner base onto template material. Repeat using the template patterns for the outer base and outer sides.

- Label the templates with the information printed on the template pattern, including the clip marks, and cut them out.

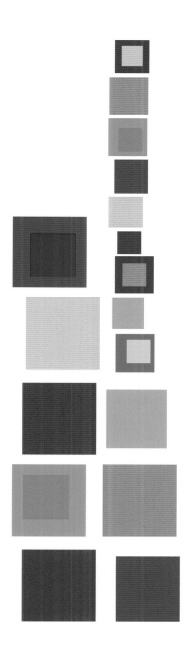

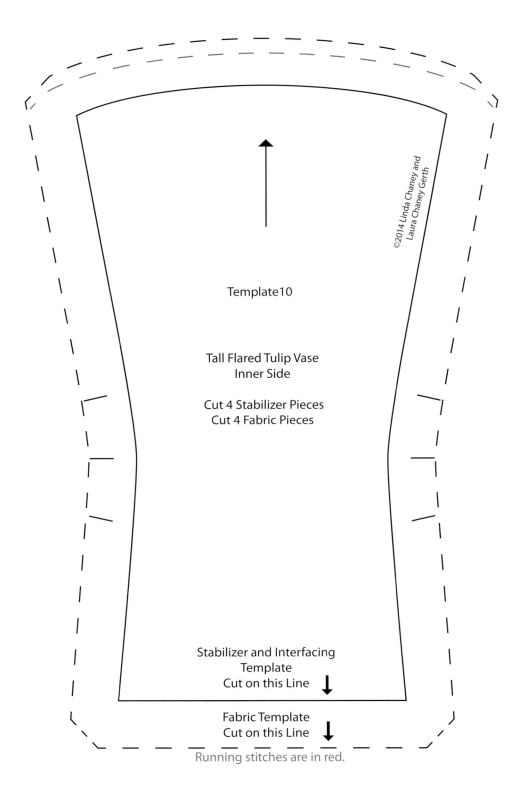

©2014 Linda Chaney and
Laura Chaney Gerth

Template10

Tall Flared Tulip Vase
Inner Side

Cut 4 Stabilizer Pieces
Cut 4 Fabric Pieces

Stabilizer and Interfacing
Template
Cut on this Line ↓

Fabric Template
Cut on this Line ↓

Running stitches are in red.

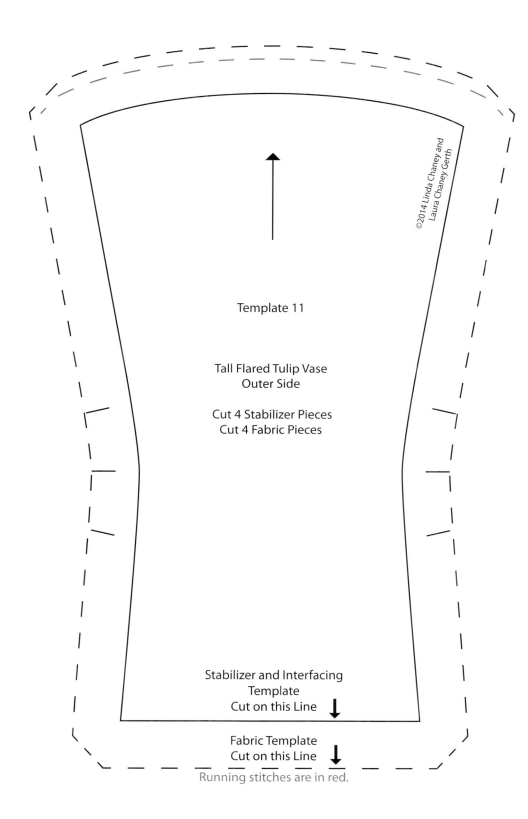

Template 11

Tall Flared Tulip Vase
Outer Side

Cut 4 Stabilizer Pieces
Cut 4 Fabric Pieces

©2014 Linda Chaney and
Laura Chaney Gerth

Stabilizer and Interfacing
Template
Cut on this Line ↓

Fabric Template
Cut on this Line ↓

Running stitches are in red.

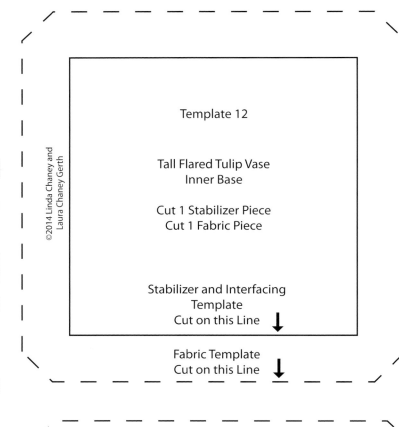

©2014 Linda Chaney and Laura Chaney Gerth

Template 12

Tall Flared Tulip Vase
Inner Base

Cut 1 Stabilizer Piece
Cut 1 Fabric Piece

Stabilizer and Interfacing
Template
Cut on this Line ↓

Fabric Template
Cut on this Line ↓

©2014 Linda Chaney and Laura Chaney Gerth

Template 13

Tall Flared Tulip Vase
Outer Base

Cut 1 Stabilizer Piece
Cut 1 Fabric Piece

Stabilizer and Interfacing
Template
Cut on this Line ↓

Fabric Template
Cut on this Line ↓

Cutting

- Using the fabric template for the inner side, cut 4 fabric pieces.

- Using the fabric template for the outer side, cut 4 fabric pieces.

- Using the fabric template for the inner base, cut 1 fabric piece.

- Using the fabric template for the outer base, cut 1 fabric piece.

- Using the stabilizer template for the inner side, cut 4 stabilizer pieces.

- Using the stabilizer template for the outer side, cut 4 stabilizer pieces.

- Using the stabilizer template for the inner base, cut 1 stabilizer piece.

- Using the stabilizer template for the outer base, cut 1 stabilizer piece.

- If embellishing the vase with embroidery, beads, or buttons, use the outer stabilizer template to cut a piece of interfacing for each outer side you want to embellish. Center the interfacing fusible-side down on the wrong side of the fabric; leave ½" of fabric uncovered on all sides, and then fuse.

LESSONS FROM LAURA

Curved edges are a little bit harder than straight edges. On curved edges I use short lengths of ¼" fusible tape to make sure I get a good clean edge around the curve. Be sure to let the piece cool for a second before you do the next side or you'll end up with burnt fingers! Try to avoid folds that may show on the edges.

Construction

- Pair the inner and outer fabrics with the inner and outer stabilizers. Work with one unit at a time.

- Sew a running stitch along the convex scalloped edges of the inner and outer sides about ⅛" from the fabric edges.

- Center a stabilizer piece on the wrong side of a fabric piece leaving ½" of fabric uncovered on all sides.

- Clip the fabric about ¼" deep at the marks on the edges of the concave outer sides and inner sides to ease the fusing of the fabric to the stabilizer.

- Apply ¼" fusible tape to one edge of a stabilizer piece. Refer to page 11 for the order in which to apply the tape.

- Slightly gather the fabric along the curved top edge by pulling on the running stitch threads.

- Fold a fabric edge over the fusible tape and the stabilizer, and fuse it to the tape one edge at a time. Make sure that the folded fabric completely covers the fusible tape to prevent the gumming of the iron. Be careful not to stretch the bias-cut edges.

- Repeat the 5 steps above until all of the stabilizer and fabric units are fused.

- Quilt the sides or base with decorative stitches, if desired.

- Lay out the octopus with right-sides up.

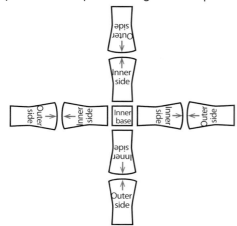

The Tall Flared Tulip Vase octopus

- Center an inner side top along an outer side top. The arrows on both pieces should point toward each other. Sew the inner side and the outer side, with the right sides together, by hand. Repeat to sew the remainder of the inner sides and outer sides together. Return the sides to their positions in the octopus. Machine and hand sewing methods are discussed on pages 13–16.

- Sew an inner side to one side of the inner base. Repeat to sew the remainder of the inner sides to the inner base.

- Sew the long side seams by hand. Have patience sewing the side seams since they are curved! Refer to page 16 for information on sewing the lip created by the joining of the outer sides and the inner sides.

- Turn the container right-side out by folding the outer sides down over the inner sides with wrong sides together. Be sure all corners and seams are fully turned and aligned.

- Turn the container upside down and lay the outer base on top of the inner base with wrong sides together.

- Align one edge of the outer base with one edge of an outer side. Use a ladder stitch or whipstitch to attach the outer base to each outer side edge.

- Backstitch to reinforce the outer base stitches at each corner. Knot and bury thread.

- Press the top edges of the container, if needed. Add embellishments, if desired, and enjoy your new vase.

Medium Concave Vases

Assembly

The construction steps are summarized below, but refer to the Tall Flared Tulip Vase instructions or the general directions on pages 9–16 for more detail.

- Using either Templates 14 and 15 flat-top vase or Templates 16 and 17 for the scalloped-top vase, trace the stabilizer and fabric template patterns for the inner sides and inner base onto template material. Repeat using either Templates 18 and 19 for the square base or Templates 20 and 21 for the hexagon base. Be sure to label the templates.

Using Templates 14–21 and the instructions for assembling the Tall Flared Tulip Vase on pages 31–35, create 2 styles of medium height vases. Pick either the flat-top side or the scalloped-top side and then choose either the square base or the hexagon base. Four different vases can be made with these templates. Isn't it wonderful to have choices?

Materials

2 fat quarters—one for the inside and one for the outside or mix and match scraps

Stabilizer—18" x 20" if using the square base or 25" x 20" if using the hexagon base

¼" fusible tape

Lightweight fusible interfacing (optional)

©2014 Linda Chaney and Laura Chaney Gerth

Template 14

Medium Flat-Top
Concave Vase
Inner Side

For Use with
the Square Base:
Cut 4 Stabilizer Pieces
Cut 4 Fabric Pieces

For Use with
the Hexagon Base:
Cut 6 Stabilizer Pieces
Cut 6 Fabric Pieces

Stabilizer and Interfacing
Template
Cut on this Line ↓

Fabric Template
Cut on this Line ↓

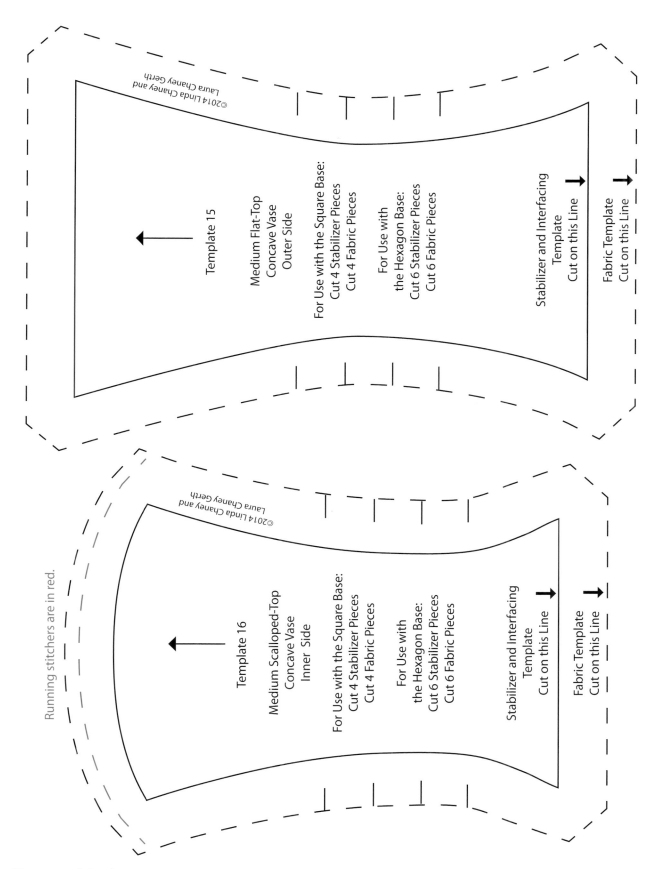

Template 15

Medium Flat-Top
Concave Vase
Outer Side

For Use with the Square Base:
Cut 4 Stabilizer Pieces
Cut 4 Fabric Pieces

For Use with
the Hexagon Base:
Cut 6 Stabilizer Pieces
Cut 6 Fabric Pieces

Stabilizer and Interfacing
Template
Cut on this Line

Fabric Template
Cut on this Line

©2014 Linda Chaney and
Laura Chaney Gerth

Template 16

Medium Scalloped-Top
Concave Vase
Inner Side

For Use with the Square Base:
Cut 4 Stabilizer Pieces
Cut 4 Fabric Pieces

For Use with
the Hexagon Base:
Cut 6 Stabilizer Pieces
Cut 6 Fabric Pieces

Stabilizer and Interfacing
Template
Cut on this Line

Fabric Template
Cut on this Line

©2014 Linda Chaney and
Laura Chaney Gerth

Running stitchers are in red.

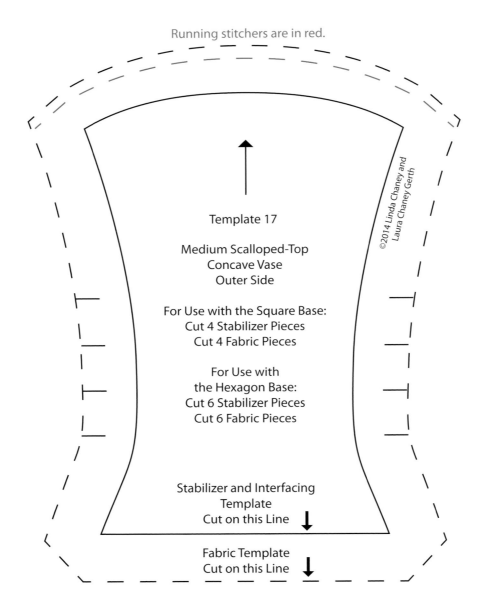

Running stitchers are in red.

Template 17

Medium Scalloped-Top
Concave Vase
Outer Side

For Use with the Square Base:
Cut 4 Stabilizer Pieces
Cut 4 Fabric Pieces

For Use with
the Hexagon Base:
Cut 6 Stabilizer Pieces
Cut 6 Fabric Pieces

Stabilizer and Interfacing
Template
Cut on this Line ↓

Fabric Template
Cut on this Line ↓

©2014 Linda Chaney and
Laura Chaney Gerth

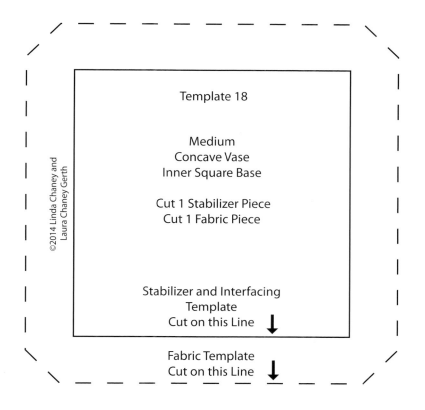

Template 18

Medium
Concave Vase
Inner Square Base

Cut 1 Stabilizer Piece
Cut 1 Fabric Piece

Stabilizer and Interfacing
Template
Cut on this Line ↓

Fabric Template
Cut on this Line ↓

©2014 Linda Chaney and
Laura Chaney Gerth

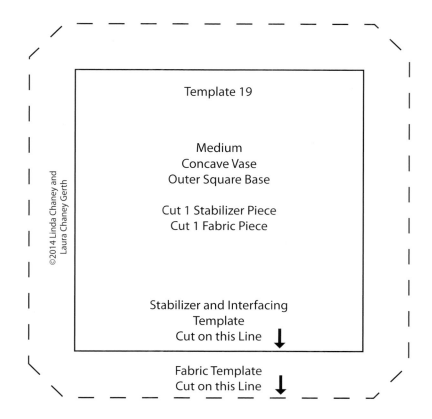

Template 19

Medium
Concave Vase
Outer Square Base

Cut 1 Stabilizer Piece
Cut 1 Fabric Piece

Stabilizer and Interfacing
Template
Cut on this Line ↓

Fabric Template
Cut on this Line ↓

©2014 Linda Chaney and
Laura Chaney Gerth

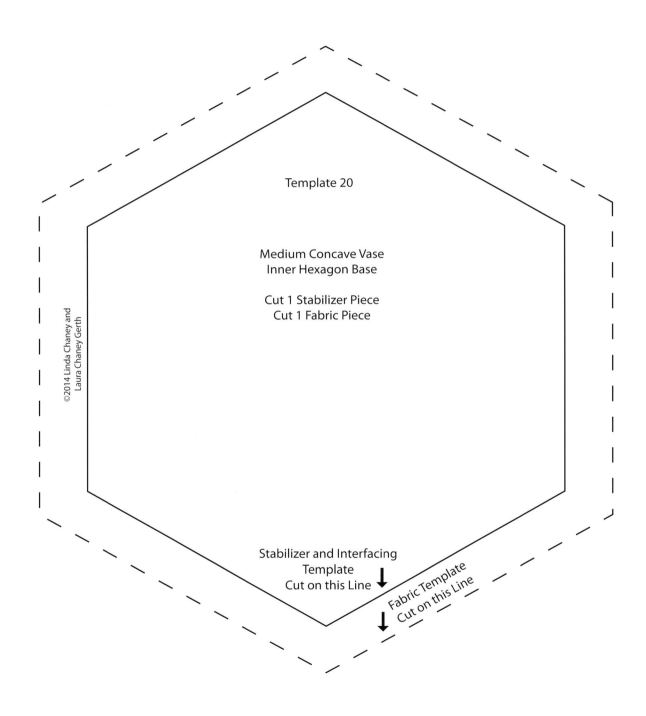

Template 20

Medium Concave Vase
Inner Hexagon Base

Cut 1 Stabilizer Piece
Cut 1 Fabric Piece

©2014 Linda Chaney and
Laura Chaney Gerth

Stabilizer and Interfacing
Template
Cut on this Line ↓

Fabric Template
Cut on this Line ↓

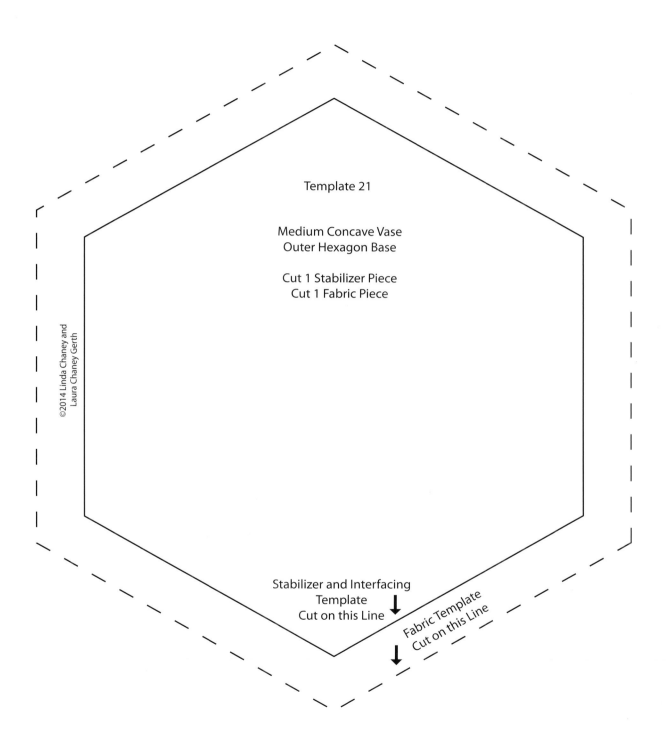

Template 21

Medium Concave Vase
Outer Hexagon Base

Cut 1 Stabilizer Piece
Cut 1 Fabric Piece

©2014 Linda Chaney and
Laura Chaney Gerth

Stabilizer and Interfacing
Template
Cut on this Line

Fabric Template
Cut on this Line

- Cut 4 fabric pieces and 4 stabilizer pieces for the inner sides and 4 fabric pieces and 4 stabilizer pieces for the outer sides if using the square base. Cut 6 fabric pieces and 6 stabilizer pieces for the inner sides and 6 fabric pieces and 6 stabilizer pieces for the outer sides if using the hexagon base.

- From either the square base or the hexagon base templates, cut 1 fabric piece and 1 stabilizer piece for the inner base and 1 fabric piece and 1 stabilizer piece for the outer base.

- When fusing the fabric to the stabilizer of the scalloped-top vases, use a running stitch along the convex curved edge as discussed on page 12.

- For completion, if you have chosen the square base for your vase, refer to the octopus for the Tall Flared Tulip Vase on page 35. If you have chosen the hexagon base for your vase, refer to the octopus below.

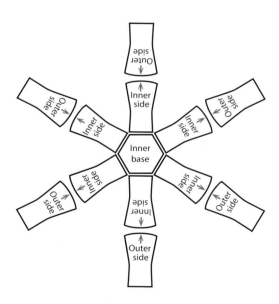

Concave Vase with a Hexagon Base octopus

Small Concave Vases

Using Templates 22–29 and the instructions for assembling the Tall Flared Tulip Vase on pages 31–35, create 2 styles of small vases. Pick either the flat-top side or the reverse scalloped-top side and then choose either the square base or the hexagon base. Four different small vases can be made with these templates. Make it your own!

Materials

2 fat quarters—one for the inside and one for the outside or mix and match scraps

Stabilizer—18" x 20" if using the square base or 25" x 20" if using the hexagon base

¼" fusible tape

Lightweight fusible interfacing (optional)

Assembly

The construction steps are the same as those for the Medium Concave Vases on pages 35–42, but refer to the Tall Flared Tulip Vase instructions on pages 31–35 or the general directions on pages 9–16 for more detail.

- Using either Templates 22 and 23 flat-top vase or Templates 24 and 25 for the reverse scalloped-top vase, trace the stabilizer and fabric template patterns for the inner sides and inner base onto template material. Repeat using either Templates 26 and 27 for the square base or Templates 28 and 29 for the hexagon base. Be sure to label the templates.

- Cut the fabric and stabilizer pieces as directed on each template.

- When fusing the fabric to the stabilizer of the scalloped-top vases, use a running stitch along the convex curved edge as discussed on page 12.

- For completion, an octopus with a square base is shown on page 35 and an octopus with a hexagon base is shown on the left.

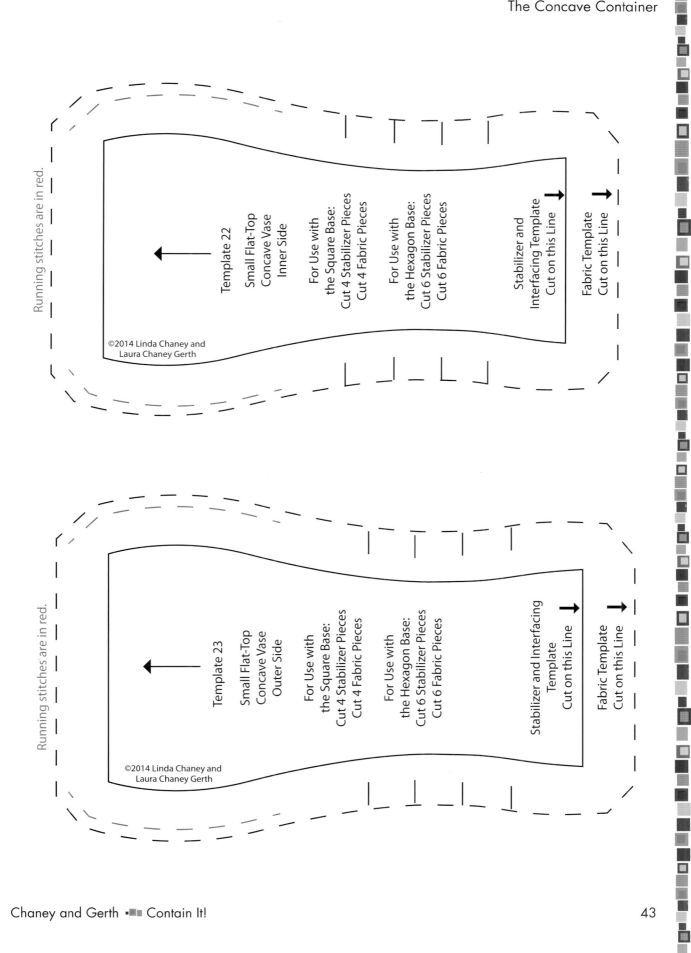

Running stitches are in red.

Template 22

Small Flat-Top
Concave Vase
Inner Side

For Use with
the Square Base:
Cut 4 Stabilizer Pieces
Cut 4 Fabric Pieces

For Use with
the Hexagon Base:
Cut 6 Stabilizer Pieces
Cut 6 Fabric Pieces

Stabilizer and
Interfacing Template
Cut on this Line

Fabric Template
Cut on this Line

©2014 Linda Chaney and
Laura Chaney Gerth

Running stitches are in red.

Template 23

Small Flat-Top
Concave Vase
Outer Side

For Use with
the Square Base:
Cut 4 Stabilizer Pieces
Cut 4 Fabric Pieces

For Use with
the Hexagon Base:
Cut 6 Stabilizer Pieces
Cut 6 Fabric Pieces

Stabilizer and Interfacing
Template
Cut on this Line

Fabric Template
Cut on this Line

©2014 Linda Chaney and
Laura Chaney Gerth

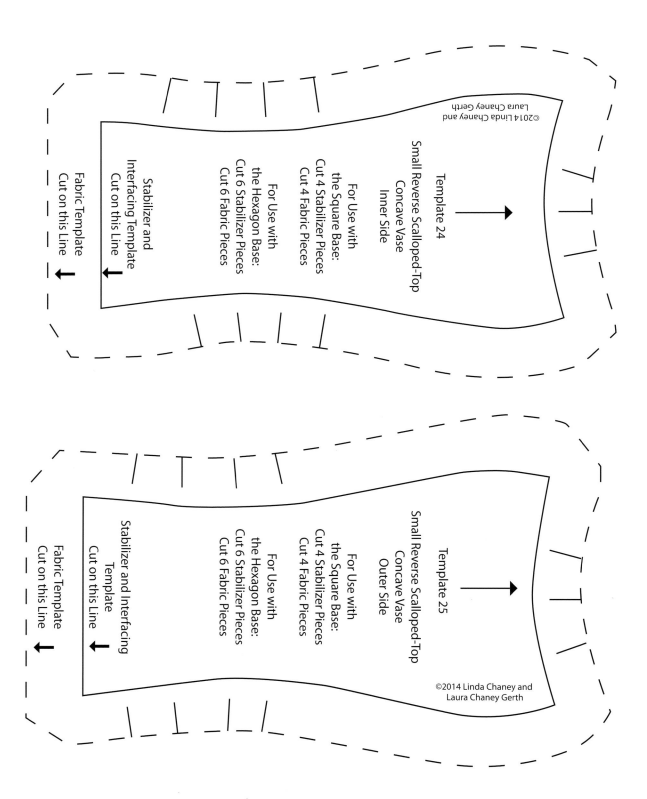

Template 24
Small Reverse Scalloped-Top
Concave Vase
Inner Side

©2014 Linda Chaney and
Laura Chaney Gerth

For Use with
the Square Base:
Cut 4 Stabilizer Pieces
Cut 4 Fabric Pieces

For Use with
the Hexagon Base:
Cut 6 Stabilizer Pieces
Cut 6 Fabric Pieces

Stabilizer and
Interfacing Template
Cut on this Line

Fabric Template
Cut on this Line

Template 25
Small Reverse Scalloped-Top
Concave Vase
Outer Side

For Use with
the Square Base:
Cut 4 Stabilizer Pieces
Cut 4 Fabric Pieces

For Use with
the Hexagon Base:
Cut 6 Stabilizer Pieces
Cut 6 Fabric Pieces

©2014 Linda Chaney and
Laura Chaney Gerth

Stabilizer and Interfacing
Template
Cut on this Line

Fabric Template
Cut on this Line

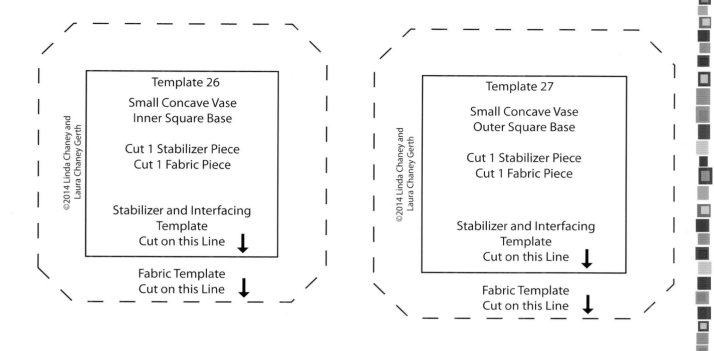

Template 26

Small Concave Vase
Inner Square Base

Cut 1 Stabilizer Piece
Cut 1 Fabric Piece

Stabilizer and Interfacing
Template
Cut on this Line ↓

Fabric Template
Cut on this Line ↓

©2014 Linda Chaney and
Laura Chaney Gerth

Template 27

Small Concave Vase
Outer Square Base

Cut 1 Stabilizer Piece
Cut 1 Fabric Piece

Stabilizer and Interfacing
Template
Cut on this Line ↓

Fabric Template
Cut on this Line ↓

©2014 Linda Chaney and
Laura Chaney Gerth

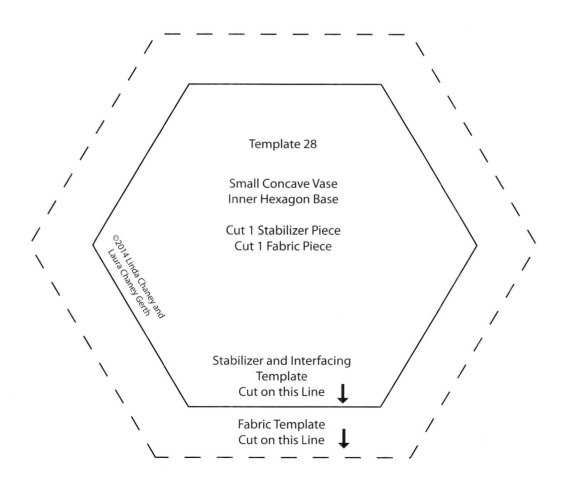

Template 28

Small Concave Vase
Inner Hexagon Base

Cut 1 Stabilizer Piece
Cut 1 Fabric Piece

©2014 Linda Chaney and
Laura Chaney Gerth

Stabilizer and Interfacing
Template
Cut on this Line ↓

Fabric Template
Cut on this Line ↓

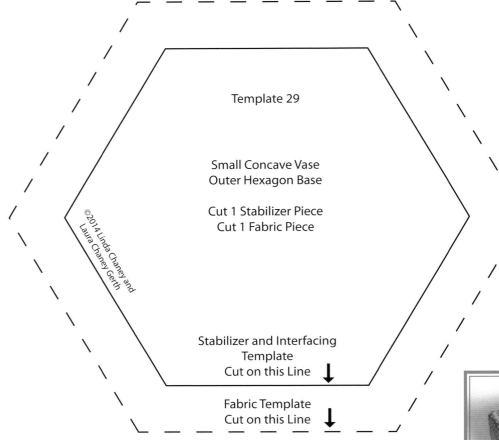

Template 29

Small Concave Vase
Outer Hexagon Base

Cut 1 Stabilizer Piece
Cut 1 Fabric Piece

©2014 Linda Chaney and
Laura Chaney Gerth

Stabilizer and Interfacing
Template
Cut on this Line ↓

Fabric Template
Cut on this Line ↓

A Gallery of Concave Vase Containers

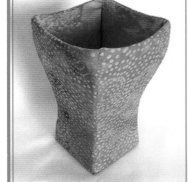

The Convex Container

Tall Convex Vase Collection

Convex containers have sides which curve outward and they make beautiful vases and bowls. There are so many things for which you can use them, from flowers to makeup brushes, or just set one on a curio shelf for an instant conversation piece. As gifts, they are guaranteed to please.

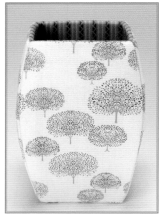

Convex vase with a square base

Convex vase with a diamond base

Convex vase with a hexagon base

This convex vase project comes with a choice of bases: square, diamond, or hexagon. The square and the diamond bases need 4 inner and 4 outer sides. The hexagon base needs 6 inner and 6 outer sides. Choosing different bases results in a wide variety of interesting (yet functional!) containers. The choice is up to you!

LESSONS FROM LAURA

To smoothly fuse the stabilizer to the fabric on convex curves, make running stitches close to and along the curved edges. Gather the fabric slightly, fold it over the fusible tape, and then press to flatten the gathers while fusing the edges to the tape.

Materials

2 fat quarters—one for the inside and one for the outside or mix and match scraps

Stabilizer—20" x 20" for the square or diamond base or 26" x 20" for the hexagon base

¼" fusible tape

Lightweight fusible interfacing (optional)

Assembly

The construction steps are summarized below, but refer to the general directions for more detail.

- Decide which base shape you wish to use—square, diamond, or hexagon.

- Use Templates 30 and 31 for the inner and outer sides. Choose Templates 32 and 33 for the square base, Templates 34 and 35 for the diamond base, or Templates 36 and 37 for the hexagon base.

- Trace the stabilizer and fabric template patterns for the inner sides and inner base onto template material. Repeat using the template patterns for the outer sides and outer base.

- Label each template with the information shown on the template patterns and cut them out.

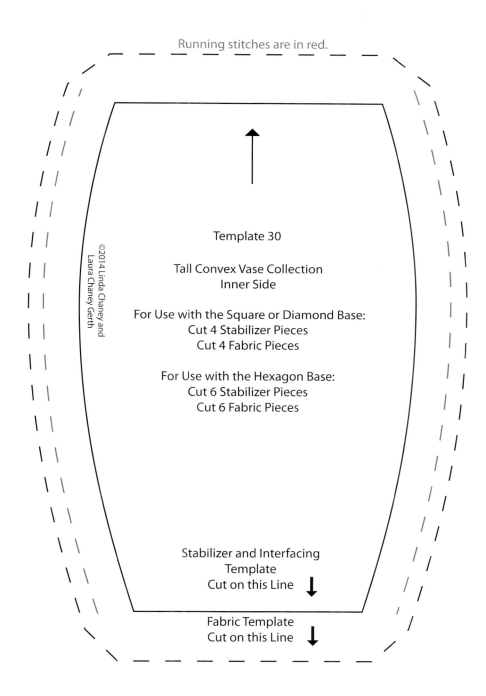

Running stitches are in red.

Template 30

Tall Convex Vase Collection
Inner Side

For Use with the Square or Diamond Base:
Cut 4 Stabilizer Pieces
Cut 4 Fabric Pieces

For Use with the Hexagon Base:
Cut 6 Stabilizer Pieces
Cut 6 Fabric Pieces

©2014 Linda Chaney and
Laura Chaney Gerth

Stabilizer and Interfacing
Template
Cut on this Line ↓

Fabric Template
Cut on this Line ↓

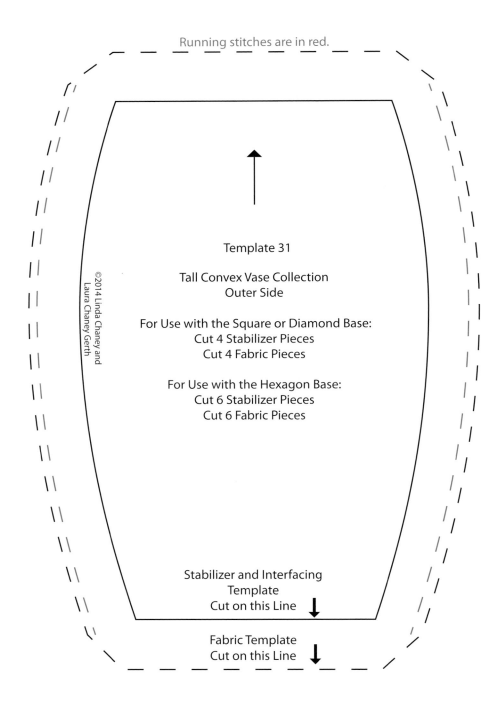

Running stitches are in red.

©2014 Linda Chaney and
Laura Chaney Gerth

Template 31

Tall Convex Vase Collection
Outer Side

For Use with the Square or Diamond Base:
Cut 4 Stabilizer Pieces
Cut 4 Fabric Pieces

For Use with the Hexagon Base:
Cut 6 Stabilizer Pieces
Cut 6 Fabric Pieces

Stabilizer and Interfacing
Template
Cut on this Line

Fabric Template
Cut on this Line

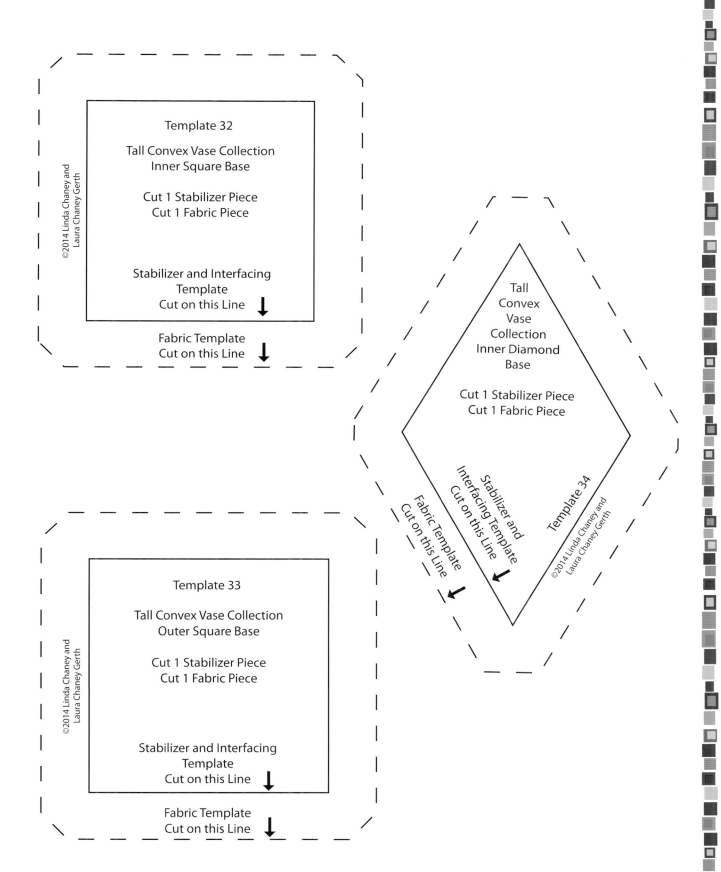

Template 32

Tall Convex Vase Collection
Inner Square Base

Cut 1 Stabilizer Piece
Cut 1 Fabric Piece

Stabilizer and Interfacing
Template
Cut on this Line ↓

Fabric Template
Cut on this Line ↓

©2014 Linda Chaney and Laura Chaney Gerth

Template 33

Tall Convex Vase Collection
Outer Square Base

Cut 1 Stabilizer Piece
Cut 1 Fabric Piece

Stabilizer and Interfacing
Template
Cut on this Line ↓

Fabric Template
Cut on this Line ↓

©2014 Linda Chaney and Laura Chaney Gerth

Tall
Convex
Vase
Collection
Inner Diamond
Base

Cut 1 Stabilizer Piece
Cut 1 Fabric Piece

Stabilizer and Interfacing Template
Cut on this Line

Fabric Template
Cut on this Line

Template 34

©2014 Linda Chaney and Laura Chaney Gerth

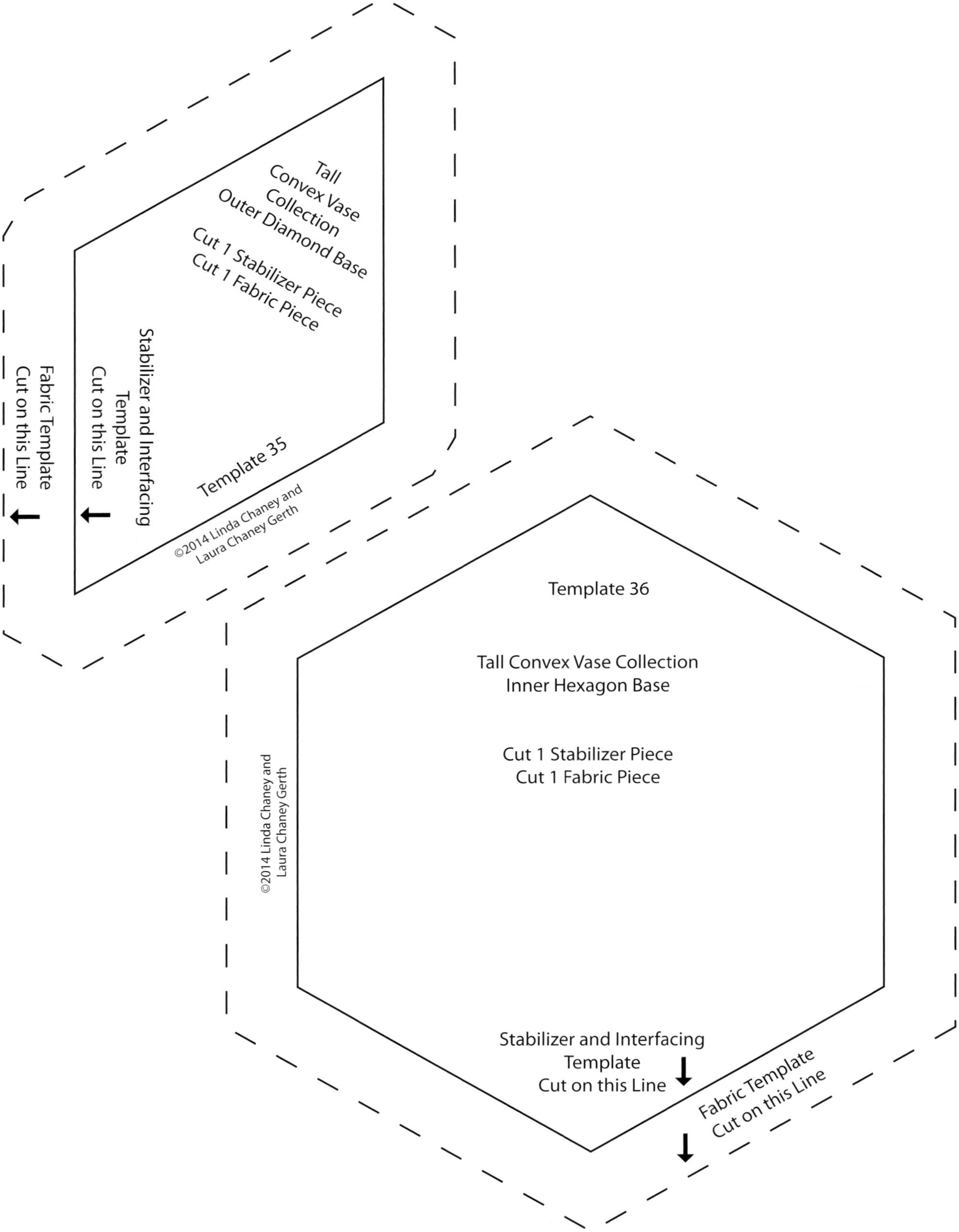

Tall
Convex Vase
Collection
Outer Diamond Base

Cut 1 Stabilizer Piece
Cut 1 Fabric Piece

Stabilizer and Interfacing
Template
Cut on this Line

Fabric Template
Cut on this Line

Template 35

©2014 Linda Chaney and
Laura Chaney Gerth

Template 36

Tall Convex Vase Collection
Inner Hexagon Base

Cut 1 Stabilizer Piece
Cut 1 Fabric Piece

©2014 Linda Chaney and
Laura Chaney Gerth

Stabilizer and Interfacing
Template
Cut on this Line

Fabric Template
Cut on this Line

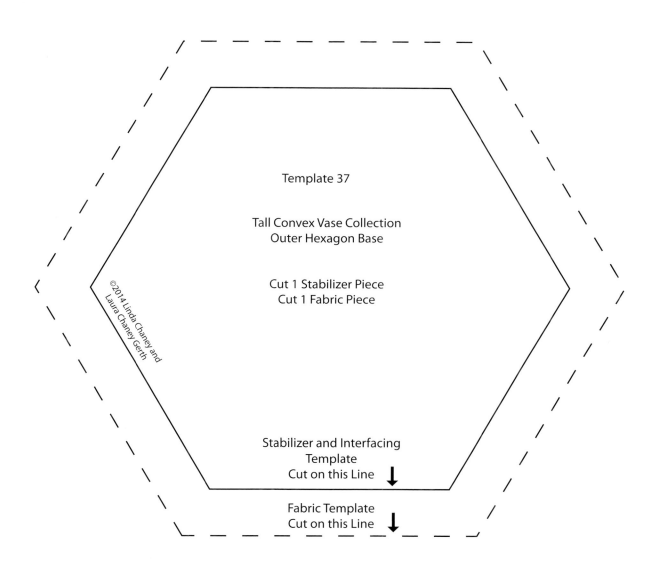

Template 37

Tall Convex Vase Collection
Outer Hexagon Base

Cut 1 Stabilizer Piece
Cut 1 Fabric Piece

©2014 Linda Chaney and
Laura Chaney Gerth

Stabilizer and Interfacing
Template
Cut on this Line ↓

Fabric Template
Cut on this Line ↓

Cutting

- Using the inner side fabric template, cut 4 fabric pieces if using the square or diamond base. Cut 6 fabric pieces if using the hexagon base.

- Using the outer side fabric template, cut 4 fabric pieces if using the square or diamond base. Cut 6 fabric pieces if using the hexagon base.

- Using the inner base template of your choice, cut 1 fabric piece.

- Using the matching outer base template, cut 1 fabric piece.

- Using the inner side stabilizer template, cut 4 stabilizer pieces if using the square or diamond base. Cut 6 stabilizer pieces if using the hexagon base.

- Using the outer side stabilizer template, cut 4 stabilizer pieces if using the square or diamond base. Cut 6 stabilizer pieces if using the hexagon base.

- Using the inner base stabilizer template that matches your chosen inner base fabric template, cut 1 stabilizer piece.

- Using the matching outer base stabilizer template, cut 1 stabilizer piece.

- If embellishing the vase with embroidery, beads, or buttons, use the outer stabilizer template to cut a piece of interfacing for each outer side you want to embellish. Center the interfacing fusible-side down on the wrong side of the fabric and leave ½" of fabric uncovered on all sides and then fuse.

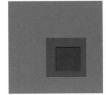

LESSONS FROM LAURA

Remember that curved edges take a little more work than straight edges. Use short lengths of ¼" fusible tape to get a good clean edge around the curve. Try to avoid folds that may show on the edges.

Construction

- Pair the inner and outer fabrics with the inner and outer stabilizers. Work with one unit at a time.

- Sew a running stitch along the convex edges of the inner and outer sides about ⅛" from the fabric edges.

- Center a stabilizer piece on the wrong side of a fabric piece leaving ½" of fabric uncovered on all sides.

- Apply ¼" fusible tape to one edge of a stabilizer piece. Refer to page 11 for the order in which to apply the tape.

- Gather the fabric slightly by gently pulling on the running-stitch threads. Fold the fabric over the fusible tape, and then press to flatten the gathers while fusing the fabric edges to the tape one edge at a time. Make sure that the folded fabric completely covers the fusible tape to prevent the gumming of the iron. Be careful not to stretch the bias-cut edges. Remove the running stitches.

- Repeat the 3 steps above until all of the stabilizer and fabric units are fused.

- Quilt the sides or base with decorative stitches, if desired.

- Lay out the octopus with right-sides up.

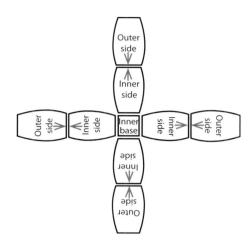

The Tall Convex Vase with a Square Base octopus

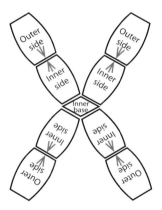

The Tall Convex Vase with a Diamond Base octopus

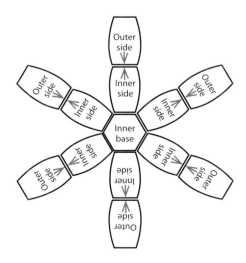

The Tall Convex Vase with a Hexagon Base octopus

- Center an inner side top along an outer side top. The arrows on both pieces should point toward each other. Sew the inner side and the outer side by machine or hand along the top edge. If sewing by hand, sew the pieces with right sides together. Repeat to sew the remainder of the inner sides and outer sides together. Return the sides to their positions in the octopus. Machine and hand sewing methods are discussed on pages 13–16.

- Sew an inner side to one side of the inner base. Repeat to sew the remainder of the inner sides to the inner base.

- Sew the long side seams by hand. Take your time in sewing the side seams since they are curved! Refer to page 16 for information on sewing the lip created by the joining of the outer sides and the inner sides.

- Turn the container right-side out by folding the outer sides down over the inner sides with wrong sides together. Be sure all corners and seams are fully turned and aligned.

- Turn the container upside down and lay the outer base on top of the inner base with wrong sides together.

- Align one edge of the outer base with one edge of an outer side. Use a ladder stitch or whipstitch to attach the outer base to each outer side edge.

- Backstitch to reinforce the outer base stitches at each corner. Knot and bury thread.

- Press the top edges of the container, if needed. Add embellishments, if desired, and enjoy your new vase.

LESSONS FROM LAURA
Try turning the finished vase upside down to create a small pedestal instead of a bowl or vase.

Medium Convex Flat-Top Vase Collection

Assembly

- Using the side and base Templates 38–45 and the instructions for assembling the Tall Convex Vase on pages 48–55, create a medium flat-top vase with your choice of a square, diamond, or pentagon base. For greater construction detail, refer to the general instructions on pages 9–16.

- Trace the inner side fabric and stabilizer templates and the outer side fabric and stabilizer templates onto template material. Cut them out and label them.

- From the inner side fabric and stabilizer templates and the outer side fabric and stabilizer templates, cut 4 fabric pieces and 4 stabilizer pieces if using the square or the diamond base. If using the pentagon base, cut 5 fabric pieces and 5 stabilizer pieces each. From your chosen inner and outer base templates, cut 1 fabric piece and 1 stabilizer piece with each.

- When fusing the stabilizer to the convex-curved edges, use a running stitch along the edge as discussed on page 12.

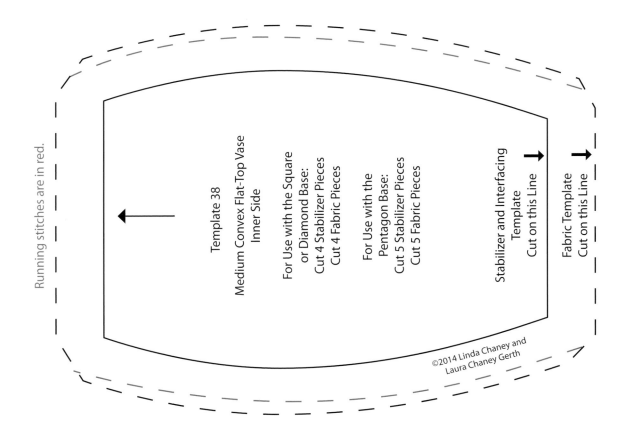

Running stitches are in red.

Template 38

Medium Convex Flat-Top Vase
Inner Side

For Use with the Square
or Diamond Base:
Cut 4 Stabilizer Pieces
Cut 4 Fabric Pieces

For Use with the
Pentagon Base:
Cut 5 Stabilizer Pieces
Cut 5 Fabric Pieces

Stabilizer and Interfacing
Template
Cut on this Line

Fabric Template
Cut on this Line

©2014 Linda Chaney and
Laura Chaney Gerth

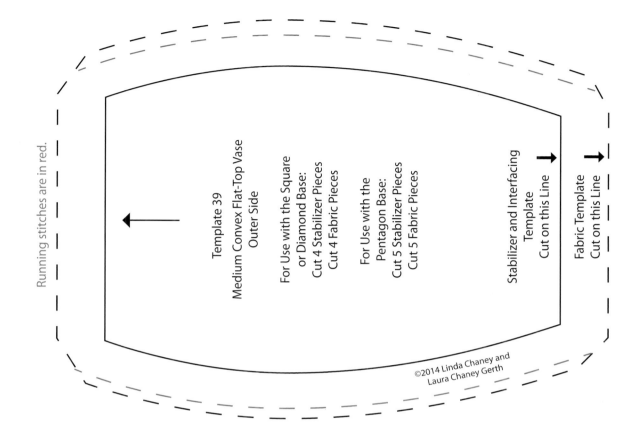

Running stitches are in red.

Template 39

Medium Convex Flat-Top Vase
Outer Side

For Use with the Square
or Diamond Base:
Cut 4 Stabilizer Pieces
Cut 4 Fabric Pieces

For Use with the
Pentagon Base:
Cut 5 Stabilizer Pieces
Cut 5 Fabric Pieces

Stabilizer and Interfacing
Template
Cut on this Line

Fabric Template
Cut on this Line

©2014 Linda Chaney and
Laura Chaney Gerth

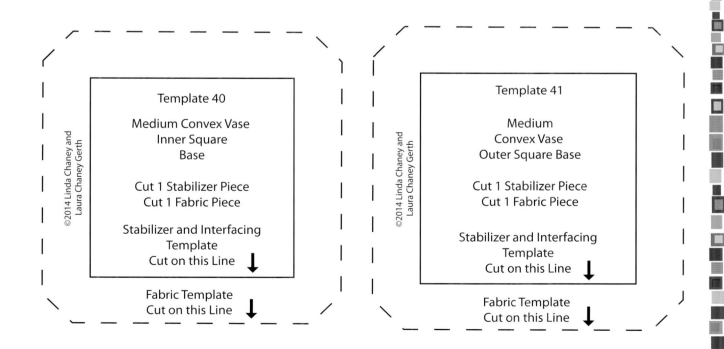

Template 40

Medium Convex Vase
Inner Square
Base

Cut 1 Stabilizer Piece
Cut 1 Fabric Piece

Stabilizer and Interfacing
Template
Cut on this Line

Fabric Template
Cut on this Line

©2014 Linda Chaney and
Laura Chaney Gerth

Template 41

Medium
Convex Vase
Outer Square Base

Cut 1 Stabilizer Piece
Cut 1 Fabric Piece

Stabilizer and Interfacing
Template
Cut on this Line

Fabric Template
Cut on this Line

©2014 Linda Chaney and
Laura Chaney Gerth

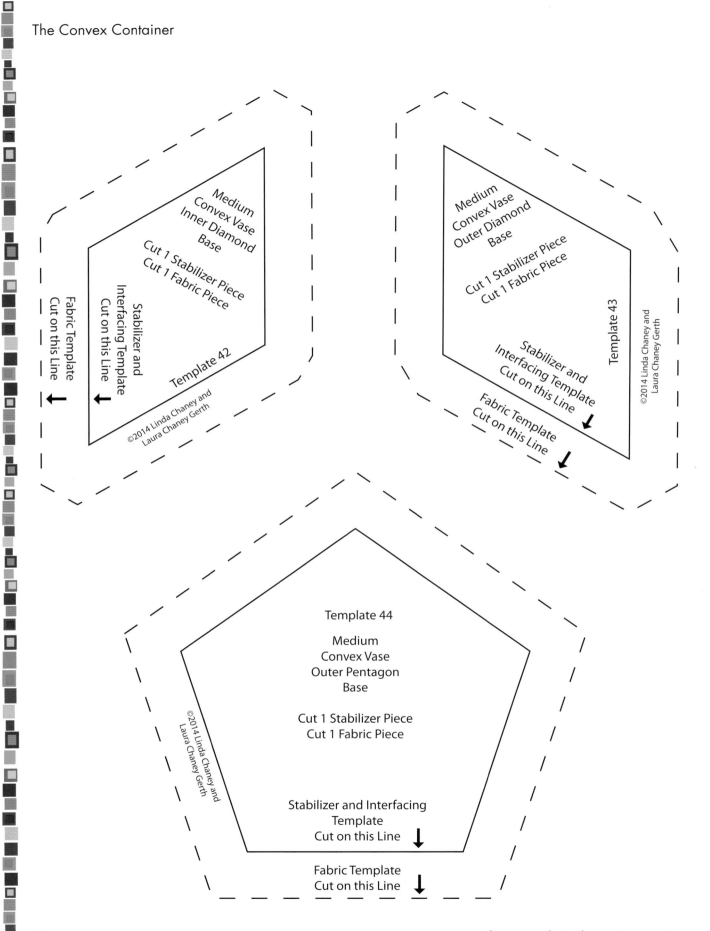

Medium
Convex Vase
Inner Diamond
Base

Cut 1 Stabilizer Piece
Cut 1 Fabric Piece

Stabilizer and
Interfacing Template
Cut on this Line

Fabric Template
Cut on this Line

Template 42

©2014 Linda Chaney and
Laura Chaney Gerth

Medium
Convex Vase
Outer Diamond
Base

Cut 1 Stabilizer Piece
Cut 1 Fabric Piece

Stabilizer and
Interfacing Template
Cut on this Line

Fabric Template
Cut on this Line

Template 43

©2014 Linda Chaney and
Laura Chaney Gerth

Template 44

Medium
Convex Vase
Outer Pentagon
Base

Cut 1 Stabilizer Piece
Cut 1 Fabric Piece

Stabilizer and Interfacing
Template
Cut on this Line

Fabric Template
Cut on this Line

©2014 Linda Chaney and
Laura Chaney Gerth

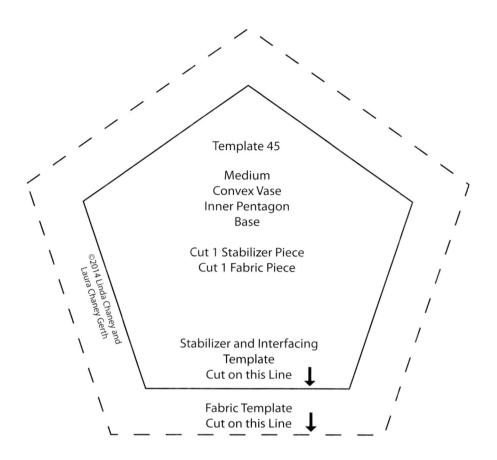

Template 45

Medium
Convex Vase
Inner Pentagon
Base

Cut 1 Stabilizer Piece
Cut 1 Fabric Piece

Stabilizer and Interfacing
Template
Cut on this Line ↓

Fabric Template
Cut on this Line ↓

©2014 Linda Chaney and
Laura Chaney Gerth

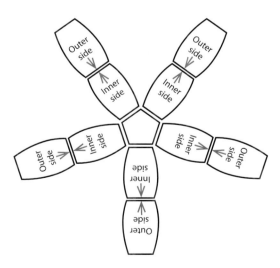

The Medium Flat-Top Convex Vase with a Pentagon Base octopus. For illustrations of octopi with square or diamond bases, refer to page 55.

Small Convex Scalloped-Top Vase Collection

Assembly

- This collection features a small scalloped-top vase with your choice of a square, diamond, or hexagon base.

- Using the side and base Templates 46–53 and the instructions for assembling the Tall Convex Vase on pages 48–55, create a small scalloped-top vase with your choice of a square, diamond, or hexagon base. For greater construction detail, refer to the general instructions on pages 9–16.

- Using Templates 46 and 47, trace the inner side fabric and stabilizer templates and the outer side fabric and stabilizer templates onto template material. For the square base, use Templates 48 and 49. For the diamond base, use Templates 50 and 51. For the hexagon base, use Templates 52 and 53. Cut the templates out and label them.

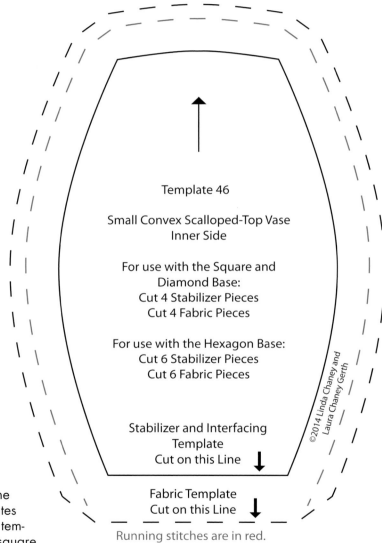

Template 46

Small Convex Scalloped-Top Vase
Inner Side

For use with the Square and
Diamond Base:
Cut 4 Stabilizer Pieces
Cut 4 Fabric Pieces

For use with the Hexagon Base:
Cut 6 Stabilizer Pieces
Cut 6 Fabric Pieces

Stabilizer and Interfacing
Template
Cut on this Line ↓

Fabric Template
Cut on this Line ↓

©2014 Linda Chaney and
Laura Chaney Gerth

Running stitches are in red.

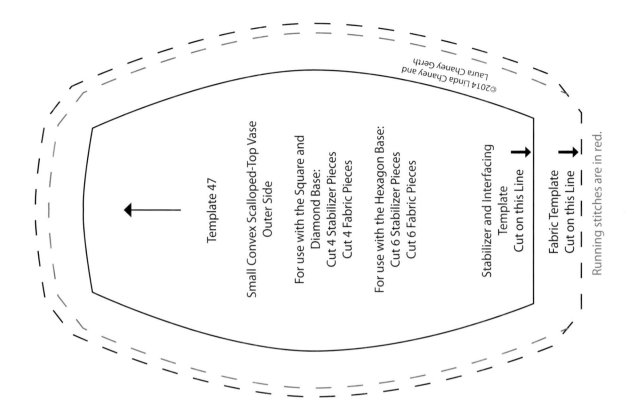

Template 47

Small Convex Scalloped-Top Vase
Outer Side

For use with the Square and
Diamond Base:
Cut 4 Stabilizer Pieces
Cut 4 Fabric Pieces

For use with the Hexagon Base:
Cut 6 Stabilizer Pieces
Cut 6 Fabric Pieces

Stabilizer and Interfacing
Template
Cut on this Line

Fabric Template
Cut on this Line

Running stitches are in red.

©2014 Linda Chaney and
Laura Chaney Gerth

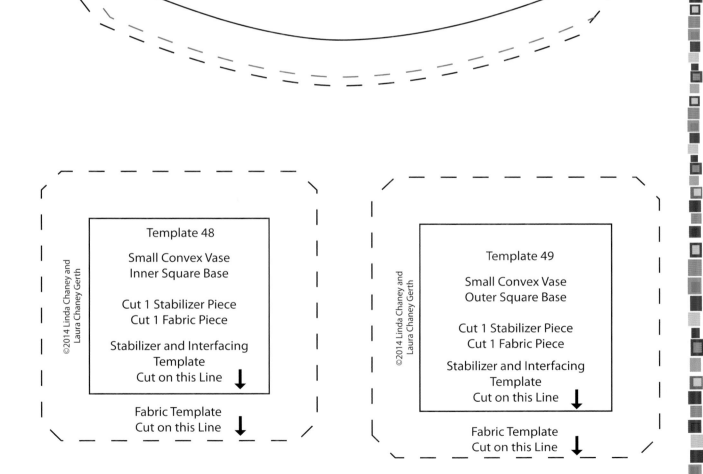

Template 48

Small Convex Vase
Inner Square Base

Cut 1 Stabilizer Piece
Cut 1 Fabric Piece

Stabilizer and Interfacing
Template
Cut on this Line

Fabric Template
Cut on this Line

©2014 Linda Chaney and
Laura Chaney Gerth

Template 49

Small Convex Vase
Outer Square Base

Cut 1 Stabilizer Piece
Cut 1 Fabric Piece

Stabilizer and Interfacing
Template
Cut on this Line

Fabric Template
Cut on this Line

©2014 Linda Chaney and
Laura Chaney Gerth

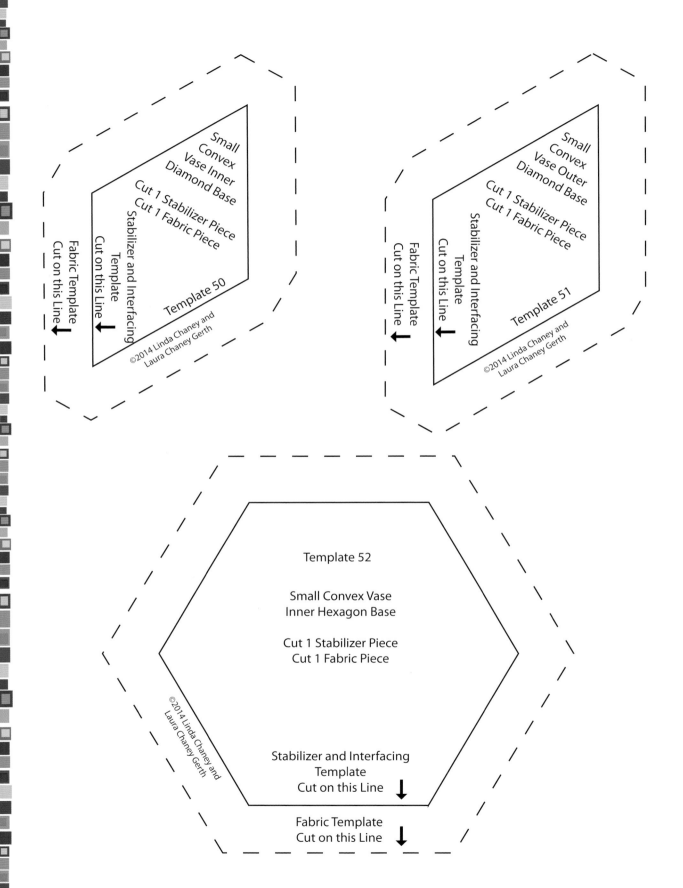

Small Convex Vase Inner Diamond Base

Cut 1 Stabilizer Piece
Cut 1 Fabric Piece

Stabilizer and Interfacing Template
Cut on this Line

Fabric Template
Cut on this Line

Template 50

©2014 Linda Chaney and Laura Chaney Gerth

Small Convex Vase Outer Diamond Base

Cut 1 Stabilizer Piece
Cut 1 Fabric Piece

Stabilizer and Interfacing Template
Cut on this Line

Fabric Template
Cut on this Line

Template 51

©2014 Linda Chaney and Laura Chaney Gerth

Template 52

Small Convex Vase
Inner Hexagon Base

Cut 1 Stabilizer Piece
Cut 1 Fabric Piece

©2014 Linda Chaney and Laura Chaney Gerth

Stabilizer and Interfacing
Template
Cut on this Line

Fabric Template
Cut on this Line

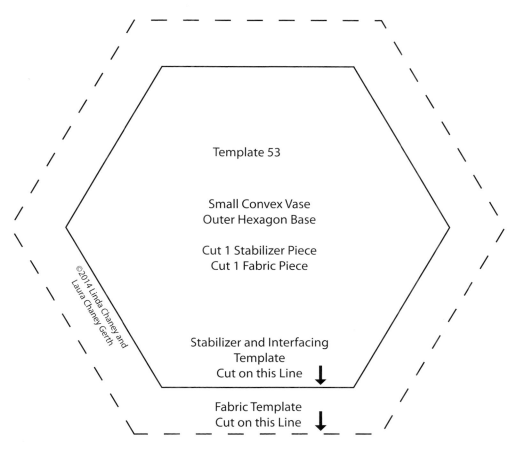

Template 53

Small Convex Vase
Outer Hexagon Base

Cut 1 Stabilizer Piece
Cut 1 Fabric Piece

©2014 Linda Chaney and
Laura Chaney Gerth

Stabilizer and Interfacing
Template
Cut on this Line ↓

Fabric Template
Cut on this Line ↓

- From the inner side fabric and stabilizer templates and the outer side fabric and stabilizer templates, cut 4 fabric pieces and 4 stabilizer pieces if using the square or the diamond base. If using the hexagon base, cut 6 fabric pieces and 6 stabilizer pieces each. From your chosen inner and outer base templates, cut 1 fabric piece and 1 stabilizer piece with each.

- When fusing the stabilizer to the convex-curved edges, use a running stitch along the edge as discussed on page 12.

- To complete construction, see page 55 for octopi with square, diamond, and hexagon bases.

A Gallery of Convex Vase Containers

The Scalloped Bowl Container

Scallops are a fun way to add a little bit of flair to a traditionally shaped bowl. You can cut the fabric to feature a specific design on each side or bottom of the scalloped bowl. This can be a great way to highlight seasonal, novelty, or holiday prints.

Scalloped Bowl Collection

This scalloped bowl project offers a choice of a square, a pentagon, or a hexagon base plus a choice of small, medium, or tall sides. The square base uses four sides to complete the bowl, the pentagon base requires five sides, and the hexagon

base needs six sides. Choose a side height and a base shape. The templates below will make 9 different bowls. The sides and bases are interchangeable; any combination will be beautiful. Perhaps you should make several—some to keep and some to share!

LESSONS FROM LAURA

Create your own fabric by sewing bits and pieces together to create a scrappy look. Select one fabric to complete the entire project or choose contrasting fabrics for various parts of the project. Fussy cutting specific design motifs will require a bit more fabric but it makes a project artistically your own.

Materials

Charm squares, fat eighths or quarters, and/or scraps

Stabilizer—For square and diamond bases, use 12" x 20" for the smallest bowl, 25" x 20" for the largest bowl.

¼" fusible tape

Lightweight fusible interfacing (optional)

Assembly

The construction steps are summarized below but refer to the general directions on pages 9–16 for more detail.

- Decide which base shape—square, pentagon, or hexagon—and which side height—small, medium, or tall—you wish to use. There are so many possibilities!

- Choose the side template for the project. You will need an inner side and an outer side.

- Choose the base template for the project. You will need an inner base and an outer base.

Template 54

Tall Scalloped Bowl
Inner Side

For Use with the Square Base:
Cut 4 Stabilizer Pieces
Cut 4 Fabric Pieces

For Use with the Pentagon Base:
Cut 5 Stabilizer Pieces
Cut 5 Fabric Pieces

For Use with the Hexagon Base:
Cut 6 Stabilizer Pieces
Cut 6 Fabric Pieces

Stabilizer and Interfacing
Template
Cut on this Line ↓

Fabric Template
Cut on this Line ↓

©2014 Linda Chaney and Laura Chaney Gerth

Running stitches are in red.

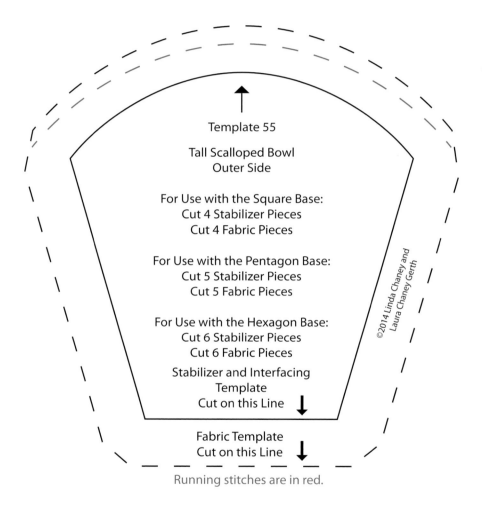

Template 55

Tall Scalloped Bowl
Outer Side

For Use with the Square Base:
Cut 4 Stabilizer Pieces
Cut 4 Fabric Pieces

For Use with the Pentagon Base:
Cut 5 Stabilizer Pieces
Cut 5 Fabric Pieces

For Use with the Hexagon Base:
Cut 6 Stabilizer Pieces
Cut 6 Fabric Pieces

Stabilizer and Interfacing
Template
Cut on this Line

Fabric Template
Cut on this Line

Running stitches are in red.

©2014 Linda Chaney and
Laura Chaney Gerth

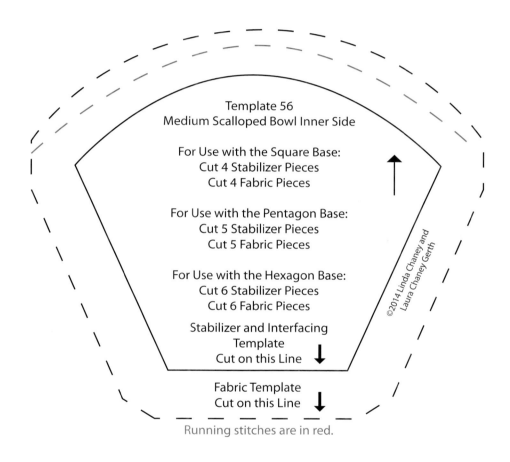

Template 56
Medium Scalloped Bowl Inner Side

For Use with the Square Base:
Cut 4 Stabilizer Pieces
Cut 4 Fabric Pieces

For Use with the Pentagon Base:
Cut 5 Stabilizer Pieces
Cut 5 Fabric Pieces

For Use with the Hexagon Base:
Cut 6 Stabilizer Pieces
Cut 6 Fabric Pieces

Stabilizer and Interfacing
Template
Cut on this Line ↓

Fabric Template
Cut on this Line ↓

Running stitches are in red.

©2014 Linda Chaney and
Laura Chaney Gerth

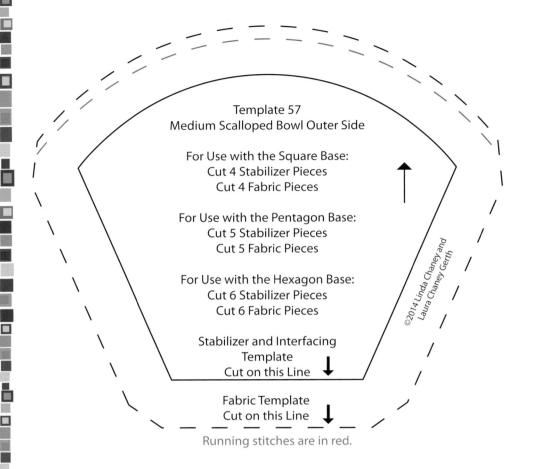

Template 57
Medium Scalloped Bowl Outer Side

For Use with the Square Base:
Cut 4 Stabilizer Pieces
Cut 4 Fabric Pieces

For Use with the Pentagon Base:
Cut 5 Stabilizer Pieces
Cut 5 Fabric Pieces

For Use with the Hexagon Base:
Cut 6 Stabilizer Pieces
Cut 6 Fabric Pieces

Stabilizer and Interfacing
Template
Cut on this Line ↓

Fabric Template
Cut on this Line ↓

©2014 Linda Chaney and Laura Chaney Gerth

Running stitches are in red.

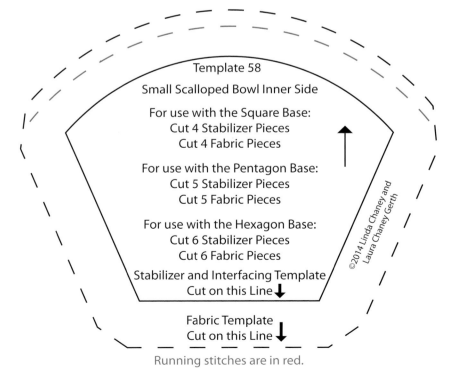

Template 58
Small Scalloped Bowl Inner Side

For use with the Square Base:
Cut 4 Stabilizer Pieces
Cut 4 Fabric Pieces

For use with the Pentagon Base:
Cut 5 Stabilizer Pieces
Cut 5 Fabric Pieces

For use with the Hexagon Base:
Cut 6 Stabilizer Pieces
Cut 6 Fabric Pieces

Stabilizer and Interfacing Template
Cut on this Line ↓

Fabric Template
Cut on this Line ↓

©2014 Linda Chaney and Laura Chaney Gerth

Running stitches are in red.

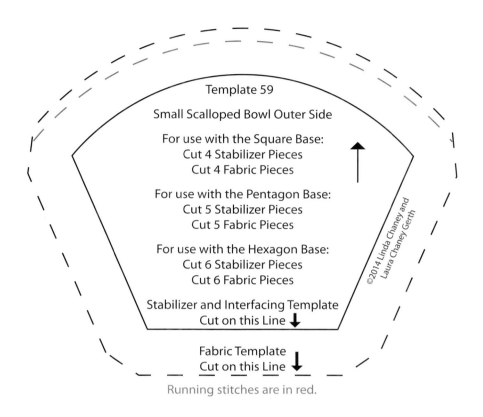

Template 59

Small Scalloped Bowl Outer Side

For use with the Square Base:
Cut 4 Stabilizer Pieces
Cut 4 Fabric Pieces

For use with the Pentagon Base:
Cut 5 Stabilizer Pieces
Cut 5 Fabric Pieces

For use with the Hexagon Base:
Cut 6 Stabilizer Pieces
Cut 6 Fabric Pieces

Stabilizer and Interfacing Template
Cut on this Line ↓

Fabric Template
Cut on this Line ↓

©2014 Linda Chaney and Laura Chaney Gerth

Running stitches are in red.

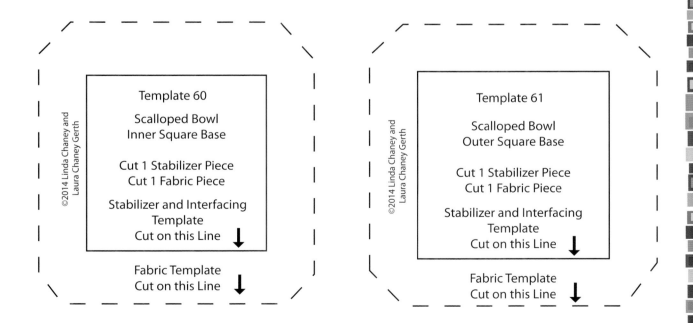

Template 60

Scalloped Bowl
Inner Square Base

Cut 1 Stabilizer Piece
Cut 1 Fabric Piece

Stabilizer and Interfacing
Template
Cut on this Line ↓

Fabric Template
Cut on this Line ↓

©2014 Linda Chaney and Laura Chaney Gerth

Template 61

Scalloped Bowl
Outer Square Base

Cut 1 Stabilizer Piece
Cut 1 Fabric Piece

Stabilizer and Interfacing
Template
Cut on this Line ↓

Fabric Template
Cut on this Line ↓

©2014 Linda Chaney and Laura Chaney Gerth

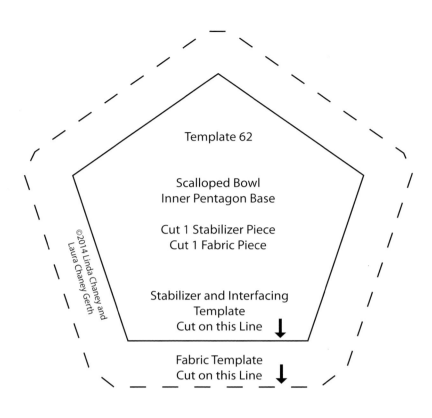

Template 62

Scalloped Bowl
Inner Pentagon Base

Cut 1 Stabilizer Piece
Cut 1 Fabric Piece

Stabilizer and Interfacing
Template
Cut on this Line

Fabric Template
Cut on this Line

©2014 Linda Chaney and
Laura Chaney Gerth

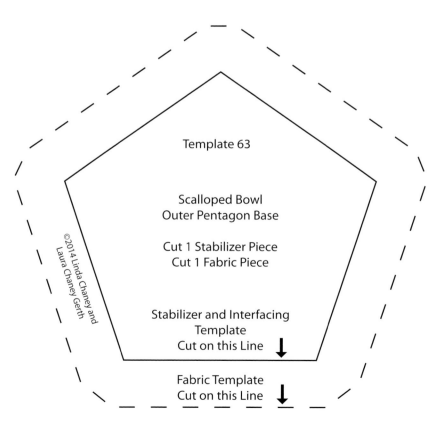

Template 63

Scalloped Bowl
Outer Pentagon Base

Cut 1 Stabilizer Piece
Cut 1 Fabric Piece

Stabilizer and Interfacing
Template
Cut on this Line

Fabric Template
Cut on this Line

©2014 Linda Chaney and
Laura Chaney Gerth

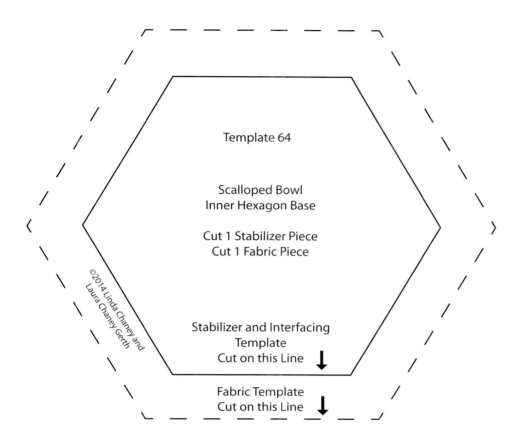

Template 64

Scalloped Bowl
Inner Hexagon Base

Cut 1 Stabilizer Piece
Cut 1 Fabric Piece

©2014 Linda Chaney and
Laura Chaney Gerth

Stabilizer and Interfacing
Template
Cut on this Line ↓

Fabric Template
Cut on this Line ↓

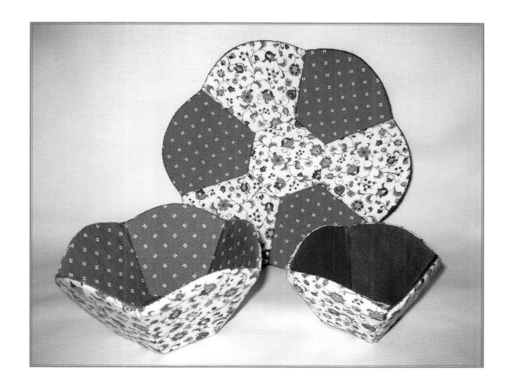

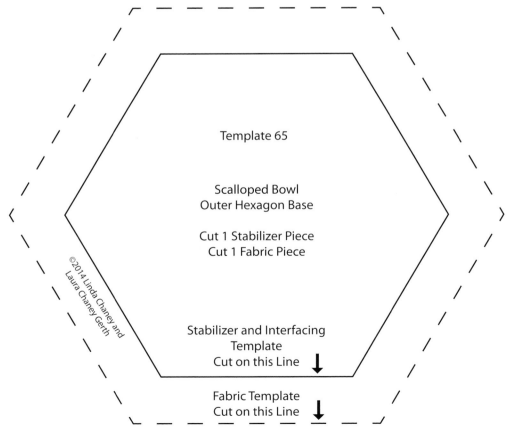

Template 65

Scalloped Bowl
Outer Hexagon Base

Cut 1 Stabilizer Piece
Cut 1 Fabric Piece

©2014 Linda Chaney and
Laura Chaney Gerth

Stabilizer and Interfacing
Template
Cut on this Line ↓

Fabric Template
Cut on this Line ↓

- Trace the chosen stabilizer and fabric template patterns for the inner sides and inner base onto template material. Repeat using the corresponding template patterns for the outer sides and outer base.

- Label each template with the information shown on the template pattern and cut them out.

Cutting

- Using the inner side fabric template of your choice, cut 4 fabric pieces if using the square base, cut 5 fabric pieces if using the pentagon base, or cut 6 fabric pieces if using the hexagon base.

- Using the matching outer side fabric template, cut 4 fabric pieces if using the square base, cut 5 fabric pieces if using the pentagon base, or cut 6 fabric pieces if using the hexagon base.

- Using the inner base fabric template shape of your choice, cut 1 fabric piece.

- Using the matching outer base fabric template, cut 1 fabric piece.

- Using the inner side stabilizer template shape of your choice, cut 4 stabilizer pieces if using the square base, cut 5 stabilizer pieces if using the pentagon base, or cut 6 stabilizer pieces if using the hexagon base.

- Using the matching outer side stabilizer template shape, cut 4 stabilizer pieces if using the square base, cut 5 stabilizer pieces if using the pentagon base, or cut 6 stabilizer pieces if using the hexagon base.

- Using the inner base stabilizer template shape of your choice, cut 1 stabilizer piece.

- Using the matching outer base stabilizer template shape, cut 1 stabilizer piece.

- If embellishing the vase with embroidery, beads, or buttons, use the outer stabilizer template to cut a piece of interfacing for each outer side you want to embellish. Center the interfacing fusible-side down on the wrong side of the fabric; leave ½" of fabric uncovered on all sides, and then fuse.

Construction

- Pair the inner and outer fabrics with the inner and outer stabilizers. Work with one unit at a time.

- Sew a running stitch along the top of the curved scalloped edges of the inner and outer sides about ⅛" from the fabric edges.

- Center a stabilizer piece on the wrong side of a fabric piece leaving ½" of fabric uncovered on all sides.

- Apply ¼" fusible tape to one edge of a stabilizer piece. Refer to page 11 for the order in which to apply the tape.

LESSONS FROM LAURA

The tops of the sides are scalloped edges and take a little more work than straight edges. Use short lengths of ¼" fusible tape to get a good clean edge around the curve. Try to avoid folds that may show on the edges.

- Gather the fabric slightly by gently pulling on the running-stitch threads. Fold the fabric over the fusible tape, and then press to flatten the gathers while fusing the fabric edges to the tape one edge at a time. Make sure that the folded fabric completely covers the fusible tape to prevent the gumming of the iron. Be careful not to stretch the bias-cut edges. Remove the running stitches.

- Repeat the 3 steps above until all of the stabilizer and fabric units are fused.

- Quilt the sides or base with decorative stitches, if desired.

- Lay out the octopus with right-sides up.

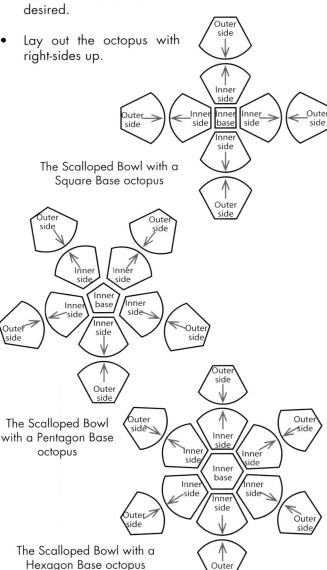

The Scalloped Bowl with a Square Base octopus

The Scalloped Bowl with a Pentagon Base octopus

The Scalloped Bowl with a Hexagon Base octopus

- Sew an inner side to one side of the inner base. Repeat to sew the remainder of the inner sides to the inner base.

- Center an inner side top along an outer side top. The arrows on both pieces should point toward

each other. Sew the inner side and the outer side, with the right sides together by hand, along the top edge. Repeat to sew the remainder of the inner sides and outer sides together. Machine and hand sewing methods are discussed on pages 13–15.

- Sew the long side seams by hand. Refer to page 16 for information on sewing the lip created by the joining of the outer sides and the inner sides.

- Turn the container right-side out by folding the outer sides down over the inner sides with wrong sides together. Be sure all corners and seams are fully turned and aligned.

- Turn the container upside down and lay the outer base on top of the inner base with wrong sides together.

- Align one edge of the outer base with one edge of an outer side. Use a ladder stitch or whipstitch to attach the outer base to each outer side edge.

- Backstitch to reinforce the outer base stitches at each corner. Knot and bury thread.

- Press the top edges of the container, if needed. Add embellishments, if desired, and enjoy your new bowl.

LESSONS FROM LAURA

To make a nested set of scallop bowls, choose a base and then make three bowls, one each with the small, the medium, and the tall sides. Stack them up. What a nice gift for a friend or to yourself!

Miniature Scalloped Bowl Collection

- Using Templates 66–77 and the instructions for assembling a scalloped bowl on pages 65–74, create a set of miniature bowls with a choice of mini, minier, and miniest heights and a choice of a square, pentagon, or hexagon base. Refer to the general directions on pages 9–16 for more detail.

- Choose the base template for the project. The miniature scalloped bowl bases fit the Mini, Minier, and Miniest sides. You will need an inner base and an outer base. The bases are on pages 78–79.

- Choose the side template for the project. You will need an inner side and an outer side.

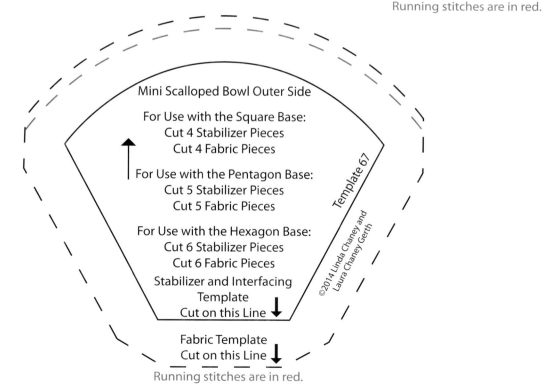

Mini Scalloped Bowl Inner Side

For Use with the Square Base:
Cut 4 Stabilizer Pieces
Cut 4 Fabric Pieces

For Use with the Pentagon Base:
Cut 5 Stabilizer Pieces
Cut 5 Fabric Pieces

For Use with the Hexagon Base:
Cut 6 Stabilizer Pieces
Cut 6 Fabric Pieces
Stabilizer and Interfacing Template
Cut on this Line ↓

Fabric Template
Cut on this Line ↓

Template 66

©2014 Linda Chaney and Laura Chaney Gerth

Running stitches are in red.

Mini Scalloped Bowl Outer Side

For Use with the Square Base:
Cut 4 Stabilizer Pieces
Cut 4 Fabric Pieces

For Use with the Pentagon Base:
Cut 5 Stabilizer Pieces
Cut 5 Fabric Pieces

For Use with the Hexagon Base:
Cut 6 Stabilizer Pieces
Cut 6 Fabric Pieces

Stabilizer and Interfacing Template
Cut on this Line ↓

Fabric Template
Cut on this Line ↓

Template 67

©2014 Linda Chaney and Laura Chaney Gerth

Running stitches are in red.

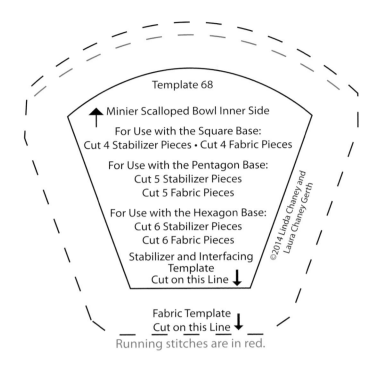

Template 68

Minier Scalloped Bowl Inner Side

For Use with the Square Base:
Cut 4 Stabilizer Pieces • Cut 4 Fabric Pieces

For Use with the Pentagon Base:
Cut 5 Stabilizer Pieces
Cut 5 Fabric Pieces

For Use with the Hexagon Base:
Cut 6 Stabilizer Pieces
Cut 6 Fabric Pieces

Stabilizer and Interfacing
Template
Cut on this Line ↓

©2014 Linda Chaney and
Laura Chaney Gerth

Fabric Template
Cut on this Line ↓

Running stitches are in red.

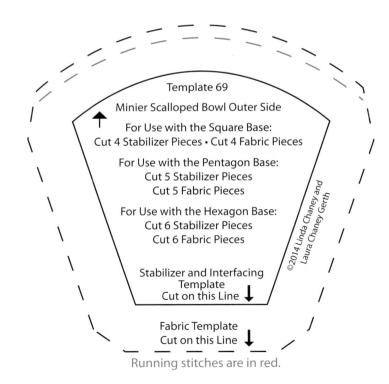

Template 69

Minier Scalloped Bowl Outer Side

For Use with the Square Base:
Cut 4 Stabilizer Pieces • Cut 4 Fabric Pieces

For Use with the Pentagon Base:
Cut 5 Stabilizer Pieces
Cut 5 Fabric Pieces

For Use with the Hexagon Base:
Cut 6 Stabilizer Pieces
Cut 6 Fabric Pieces

Stabilizer and Interfacing
Template
Cut on this Line ↓

©2014 Linda Chaney and
Laura Chaney Gerth

Fabric Template
Cut on this Line ↓

Running stitches are in red.

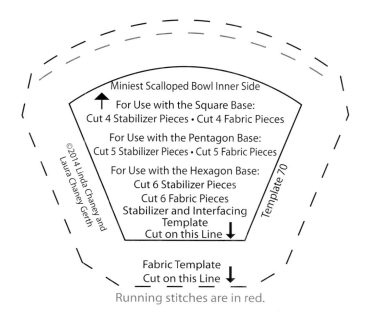

Miniest Scalloped Bowl Inner Side

For Use with the Square Base:
Cut 4 Stabilizer Pieces • Cut 4 Fabric Pieces

For Use with the Pentagon Base:
Cut 5 Stabilizer Pieces • Cut 5 Fabric Pieces

For Use with the Hexagon Base:
Cut 6 Stabilizer Pieces
Cut 6 Fabric Pieces
Stabilizer and Interfacing
Template
Cut on this Line ↓

Template 70

©2014 Linda Chaney and
Laura Chaney Gerth

Fabric Template
Cut on this Line ↓

Running stitches are in red.

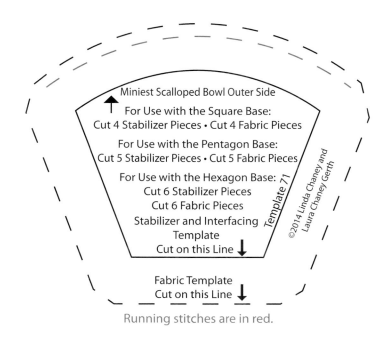

Miniest Scalloped Bowl Outer Side

For Use with the Square Base:
Cut 4 Stabilizer Pieces • Cut 4 Fabric Pieces

For Use with the Pentagon Base:
Cut 5 Stabilizer Pieces • Cut 5 Fabric Pieces

For Use with the Hexagon Base:
Cut 6 Stabilizer Pieces
Cut 6 Fabric Pieces
Stabilizer and Interfacing
Template
Cut on this Line ↓

Template 71

©2014 Linda Chaney and
Laura Chaney Gerth

Fabric Template
Cut on this Line ↓

Running stitches are in red.

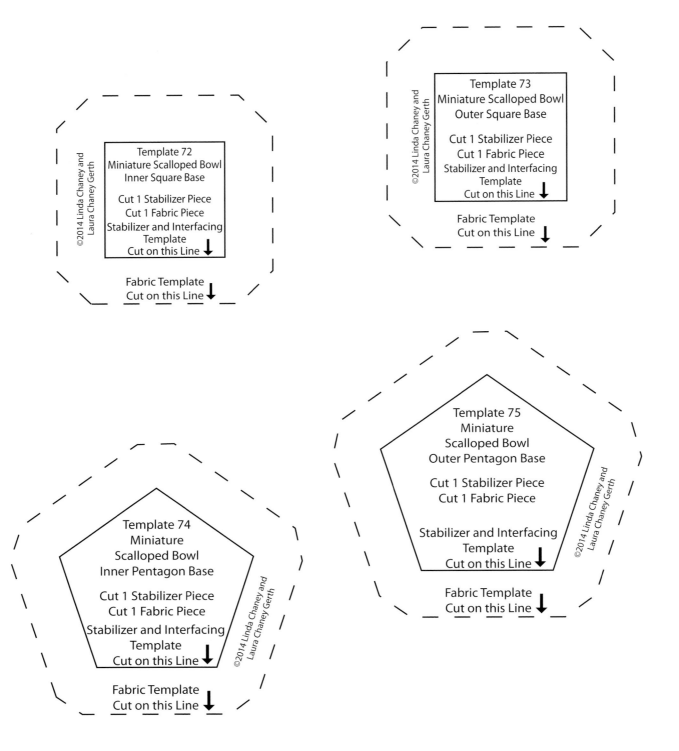

Template 72
Miniature Scalloped Bowl
Inner Square Base

Cut 1 Stabilizer Piece
Cut 1 Fabric Piece
Stabilizer and Interfacing
Template
Cut on this Line ↓

Fabric Template
Cut on this Line ↓

©2014 Linda Chaney and Laura Chaney Gerth

Template 73
Miniature Scalloped Bowl
Outer Square Base

Cut 1 Stabilizer Piece
Cut 1 Fabric Piece
Stabilizer and Interfacing
Template
Cut on this Line ↓

Fabric Template
Cut on this Line ↓

©2014 Linda Chaney and Laura Chaney Gerth

Template 74
Miniature
Scalloped Bowl
Inner Pentagon Base

Cut 1 Stabilizer Piece
Cut 1 Fabric Piece

Stabilizer and Interfacing
Template
Cut on this Line ↓

Fabric Template
Cut on this Line ↓

©2014 Linda Chaney and Laura Chaney Gerth

Template 75
Miniature
Scalloped Bowl
Outer Pentagon Base

Cut 1 Stabilizer Piece
Cut 1 Fabric Piece

Stabilizer and Interfacing
Template
Cut on this Line ↓

Fabric Template
Cut on this Line ↓

©2014 Linda Chaney and Laura Chaney Gerth

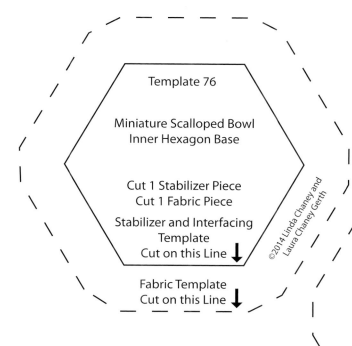

Template 76

Miniature Scalloped Bowl
Inner Hexagon Base

Cut 1 Stabilizer Piece
Cut 1 Fabric Piece

Stabilizer and Interfacing
Template
Cut on this Line ↓

Fabric Template
Cut on this Line ↓

©2014 Linda Chaney and Laura Chaney Gerth

Template 77

Miniature Scalloped Bowl
Outer Hexagon Base

Cut 1 Stabilizer Piece
Cut 1 Fabric Piece

Stabilizer and Interfacing
Template
Cut on this Line ↓

Fabric Template
Cut on this Line ↓

©2014 Linda Chaney and Laura Chaney Gerth

Assembly

- The miniature bowls are constructed just like the Scalloped Bowls at the beginning of this chapter; they are just a tinier version.

- Trace the chosen templates onto template material to make fabric and stabilizer templates. Label all templates.

- Cut the number of fabric and stabilizer pieces to match the chosen base. The bases fit all three bowl sizes. The square base will need 4 sides, the pentagon will need 5 sides, and the hexagon base will need 6 sides.

- Follow the instructions on pages 65–74 for the Scalloped Bowl Collection to complete the construction of the miniature bowls.

A Gallery of Scalloped Bowl Containers

The Heart Container

The heart-shaped box is so fun and beautiful to create. Although the hearts might seem complex to construct, they really do come together easily. These make lovely gift boxes, especially for your sweetheart or the important women in your life. You might even want a set just for you!

Heart-Shaped Box

You can use the small heart and the large heart individually or the large heart turned over the small heart to make a box!

Materials

Approximately 1 yard of assorted coordinating fabrics and/or scraps to make both hearts

Stabilizer—20" x 28"

¼" fusible tape

Lightweight fusible interfacing (optional)

LESSONS FROM LAURA

You can add a heart-shaped bowl, approximately 2¼" x 6⅛" x 5¾", that is readily available at your local dollar store. Place the bowl inside the smaller heart-shaped container and flip the slightly larger heart over it to create a box ready to fill with chocolate or other goodies.

General Assembly

- The construction steps are summarized below, but refer to the general directions on pages 9–16 for more detail.

Assembly for the Bases

- Trace the stabilizer and fabric templates for the inner square base, outer square base, inner trapezoid base, and outer trapezoid base of the small heart onto template material. Repeat using the templates for the inner square base, outer square base, inner trapezoid base, and outer trapezoid base for the large heart. Carefully label each template with the information shown on the template pattern and cut them out.

©2014 Linda Chaney and Laura Chaney Gerth

Template 78

Small Heart
Inner Square Base

Cut 1 Stabilizer Piece
Cut 1 Fabric Piece

Stabilizer and Interfacing
Template
Cut on this Line ↓

Fabric Template
Cut on this Line ↓

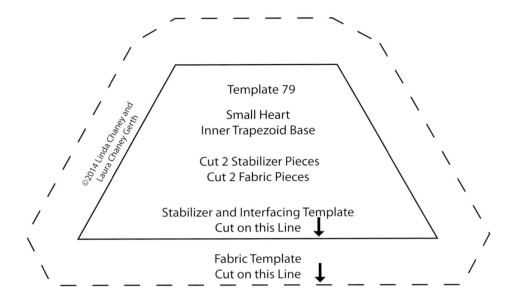

Template 79

Small Heart
Inner Trapezoid Base

Cut 2 Stabilizer Pieces
Cut 2 Fabric Pieces

Stabilizer and Interfacing Template
Cut on this Line ↓

Fabric Template
Cut on this Line ↓

©2014 Linda Chaney and
Laura Chaney Gerth

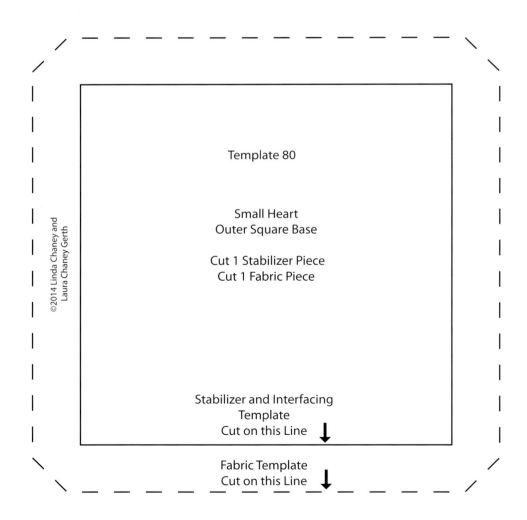

Template 80

Small Heart
Outer Square Base

Cut 1 Stabilizer Piece
Cut 1 Fabric Piece

Stabilizer and Interfacing
Template
Cut on this Line ↓

Fabric Template
Cut on this Line ↓

©2014 Linda Chaney and
Laura Chaney Gerth

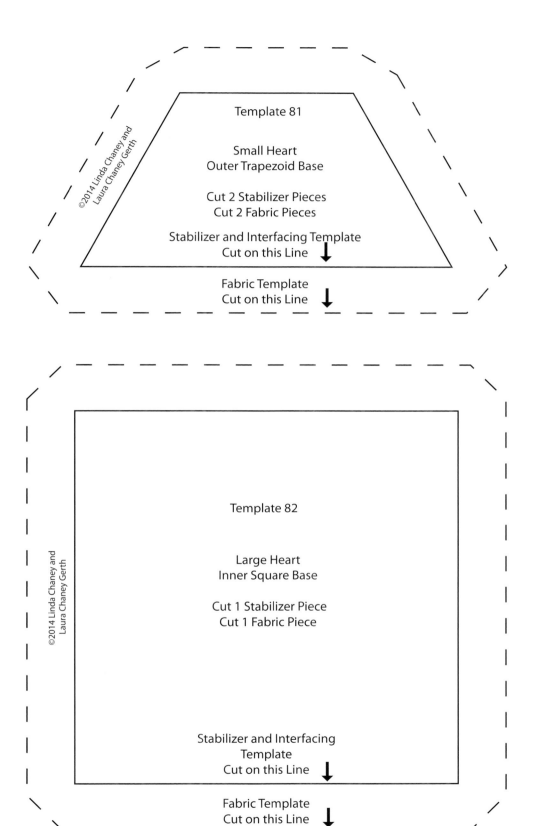

Template 81

Small Heart
Outer Trapezoid Base

Cut 2 Stabilizer Pieces
Cut 2 Fabric Pieces

Stabilizer and Interfacing Template
Cut on this Line ↓

Fabric Template
Cut on this Line ↓

©2014 Linda Chaney and
Laura Chaney Gerth

Template 82

Large Heart
Inner Square Base

Cut 1 Stabilizer Piece
Cut 1 Fabric Piece

Stabilizer and Interfacing
Template
Cut on this Line ↓

Fabric Template
Cut on this Line ↓

©2014 Linda Chaney and
Laura Chaney Gerth

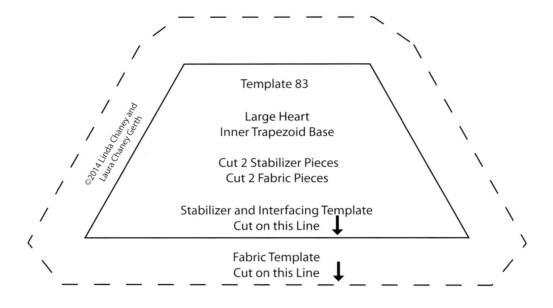

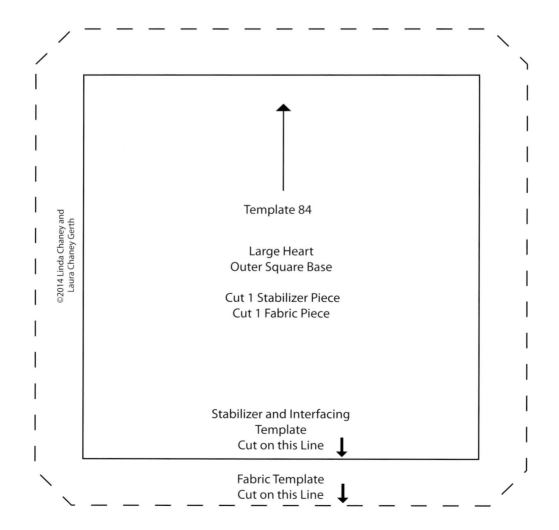

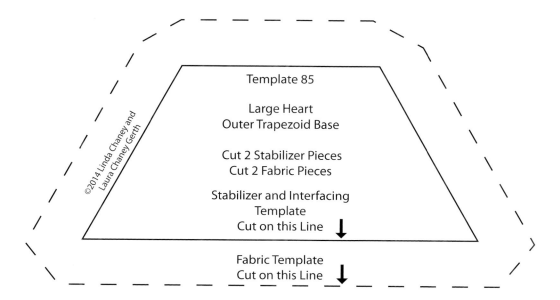

Template 85

Large Heart
Outer Trapezoid Base

Cut 2 Stabilizer Pieces
Cut 2 Fabric Pieces

Stabilizer and Interfacing
Template
Cut on this Line ↓

Fabric Template
Cut on this Line ↓

©2014 Linda Chaney and
Laura Chaney Gerth

- Using the inner square base fabric templates and outer square base fabric templates for the small heart and the large heart, cut 1 fabric piece from each template.

- Using the inner trapezoid base fabric templates and outer trapezoid base fabric templates for the small heart and the large heart, cut 2 fabric pieces from each template. Be sure to label each piece with the information on the template to avoid confusion.

- Using the inner square base stabilizer templates and outer square base stabilizer templates for the small heart and the large heart, cut 1 stabilizer piece from each template.

- Using the inner trapezoid base stabilizer templates and outer trapezoid base stabilizer templates for

the small heart and the large heart, cut 2 stabilizer pieces from each template. Be sure to label each piece with the information on the template to avoid confusion.

Assembly for the Sides

- Trace the stabilizer and fabric templates for the inner and outer sides of the small heart and the inner and outer sides of the large heart onto template material. Carefully label each template with the information shown on the template and cut them out.

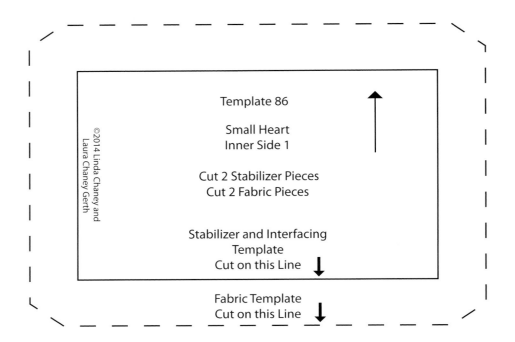

Template 86

Small Heart
Inner Side 1

Cut 2 Stabilizer Pieces
Cut 2 Fabric Pieces

Stabilizer and Interfacing
Template
Cut on this Line

Fabric Template
Cut on this Line

©2014 Linda Chaney and
Laura Chaney Gerth

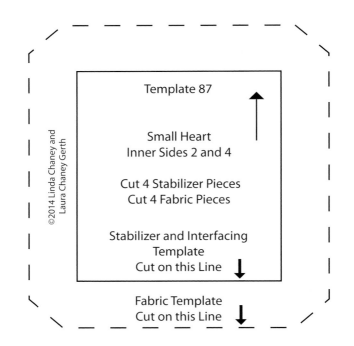

Template 87

Small Heart
Inner Sides 2 and 4

Cut 4 Stabilizer Pieces
Cut 4 Fabric Pieces

Stabilizer and Interfacing
Template
Cut on this Line

Fabric Template
Cut on this Line

©2014 Linda Chaney and
Laura Chaney Gerth

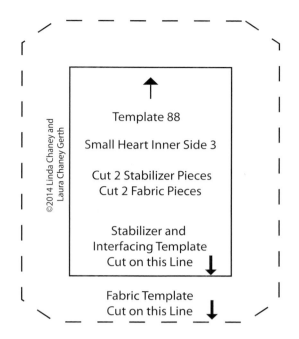

Template 88

Small Heart Inner Side 3

Cut 2 Stabilizer Pieces
Cut 2 Fabric Pieces

Stabilizer and
Interfacing Template
Cut on this Line

Fabric Template
Cut on this Line

©2014 Linda Chaney and
Laura Chaney Gerth

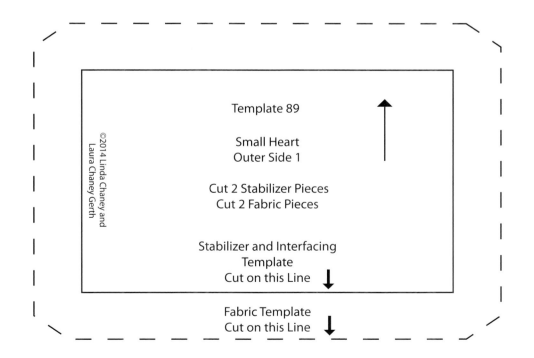

Template 89

Small Heart
Outer Side 1

Cut 2 Stabilizer Pieces
Cut 2 Fabric Pieces

Stabilizer and Interfacing
Template
Cut on this Line

Fabric Template
Cut on this Line

©2014 Linda Chaney and
Laura Chaney Gerth

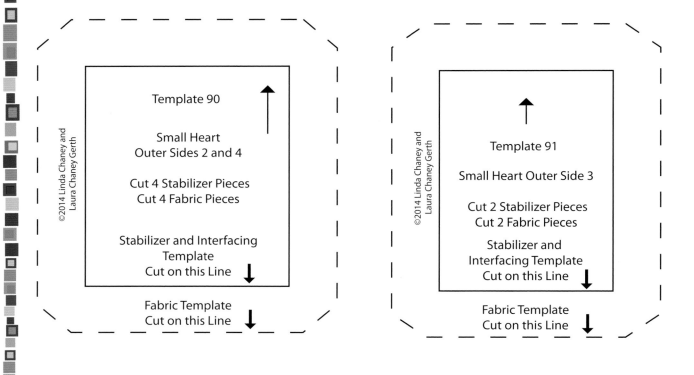

©2014 Linda Chaney and
Laura Chaney Gerth

Template 90

Small Heart
Outer Sides 2 and 4

Cut 4 Stabilizer Pieces
Cut 4 Fabric Pieces

Stabilizer and Interfacing
Template
Cut on this Line

Fabric Template
Cut on this Line

©2014 Linda Chaney and
Laura Chaney Gerth

Template 91

Small Heart Outer Side 3

Cut 2 Stabilizer Pieces
Cut 2 Fabric Pieces

Stabilizer and
Interfacing Template
Cut on this Line

Fabric Template
Cut on this Line

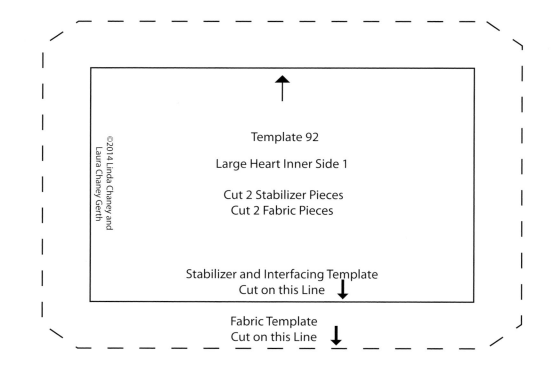

©2014 Linda Chaney and
Laura Chaney Gerth

Template 92

Large Heart Inner Side 1

Cut 2 Stabilizer Pieces
Cut 2 Fabric Pieces

Stabilizer and Interfacing Template
Cut on this Line

Fabric Template
Cut on this Line

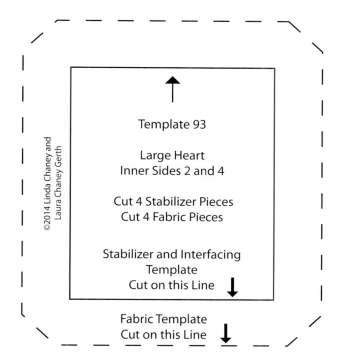

Template 93

Large Heart
Inner Sides 2 and 4

Cut 4 Stabilizer Pieces
Cut 4 Fabric Pieces

Stabilizer and Interfacing
Template
Cut on this Line

Fabric Template
Cut on this Line

©2014 Linda Chaney and
Laura Chaney Gerth

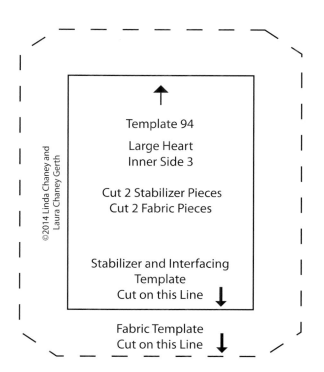

Template 94

Large Heart
Inner Side 3

Cut 2 Stabilizer Pieces
Cut 2 Fabric Pieces

Stabilizer and Interfacing
Template
Cut on this Line

Fabric Template
Cut on this Line

©2014 Linda Chaney and
Laura Chaney Gerth

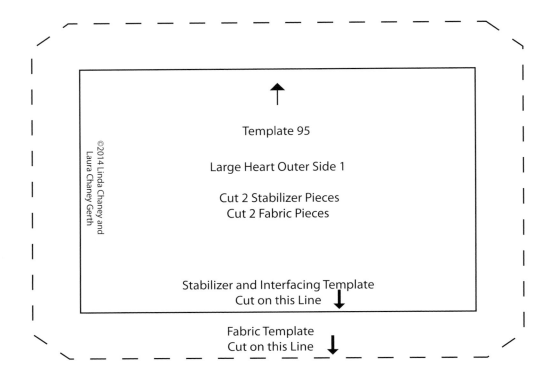

Template 95

Large Heart Outer Side 1

Cut 2 Stabilizer Pieces
Cut 2 Fabric Pieces

©2014 Linda Chaney and
Laura Chaney Gerth

Stabilizer and Interfacing Template
Cut on this Line ↓

Fabric Template
Cut on this Line ↓

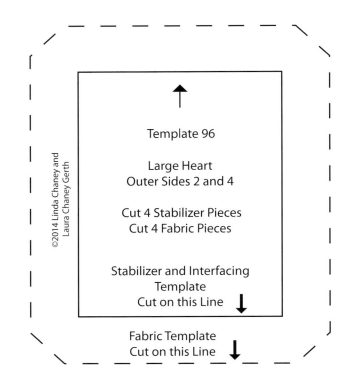

Template 96

Large Heart
Outer Sides 2 and 4

Cut 4 Stabilizer Pieces
Cut 4 Fabric Pieces

©2014 Linda Chaney and
Laura Chaney Gerth

Stabilizer and Interfacing
Template
Cut on this Line ↓

Fabric Template
Cut on this Line ↓

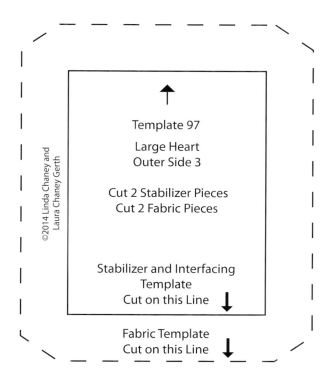

©2014 Linda Chaney and Laura Chaney Gerth

Template 97

Large Heart
Outer Side 3

Cut 2 Stabilizer Pieces
Cut 2 Fabric Pieces

Stabilizer and Interfacing
Template
Cut on this Line

Fabric Template
Cut on this Line

Cutting

- Cut 2 fabric pieces for each of the small heart inner side 1 and inner side 3 fabric templates and the small heart outer side 1 and outer side 3 fabric templates. Cut 4 fabric pieces for the small heart inner sides 2 and 4 template and the small heart outer sides 2 and 4 template. Repeat this step for the large heart using the large heart templates. This will create 32 side fabric pieces—16 for the small heart and 16 for the large heart. Be sure to label each piece with the information on the template, including arrows, to avoid confusion.

- Cut 2 stabilizer pieces for each of the small heart inner side 1 and inner side 3 stabilizer templates and the small heart outer side 1 and outer side 3 stabilizer templates. Cut 4 stabilizer pieces for the small heart inner sides 2 and 4 template and the small heart outer sides 2 and 4 template. Repeat this step for the large heart using the large heart templates. This will create 32 side stabilizer pieces—16 for the small heart and 16 for the large heart. Be sure to label each piece with the information on the template, including arrows, to avoid confusion.

Assembly for the Heart Box

- If embellishing the large heart with embroidery, beads, or buttons, use the large heart inner base and outer base stabilizer templates and the large heart outer side stabilizer templates to cut a piece of interfacing for the bases or sides you want to embellish. Center the interfacing fusible-side down on the wrong side of the fabric leaving ½" of fabric uncovered on all sides, and then fuse.

- If embellishing the small heart with embroidery, beads, or buttons, use the small heart inner base and outer base stabilizer templates and the small heart inner side stabilizer templates to cut a piece of interfacing for the bases or sides you want to embellish. The outer base of the small heart is a good place to sign your work so consider applying interfacing to this surface. Center the interfacing fusible-side down on the wrong side of the fabric leaving ½" of fabric uncovered on all sides, and then fuse.

- Pair each fabric piece with its corresponding stabilizer piece.

- Fuse one pair at a time until all of the stabilizer and fabric units are fused.

- Center a stabilizer piece on the wrong side of a fabric piece leaving ½" of the fabric uncovered on all sides.

- Apply ¼" fusible tape to one edge of a stabilizer piece. Refer to page 11 for the order in which to apply the tape.

- Fold a fabric edge over the fusible tape and the stabilizer and fuse it to the tape one side at a time. Make sure that the folded fabric completely covers the fusible tape to prevent the gumming of the iron. Be careful not to stretch the bias-cut edges.

- The small heart's outer base will become the bottom of the heart-shaped box. Sign and date your work here or quilt this piece with decorative stitches, if desired.

- Quilt the large heart outer sides or outer base with decorative stitches, if desired.

- Lay out the octopus for the small heart right-sides up and then lay out the octopus for the large heart right-sides up.

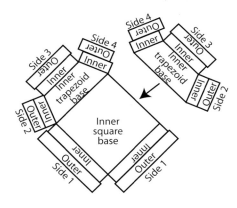

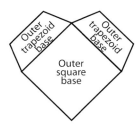

The Heart octopus

- Beginning with the small heart, pair an inner side 4 and an outer side 4 by placing the outer side 4 slightly offset over the inner side 4 as shown in the diagram below. The left outer side 4 is offset by ⅟₁₆" to the left of inner side 4. The right outer side 4 is offset by ⅟₁₆" to the right of inner side 4. Sew each pair with the right sides together while maintaining the ⅟₁₆" offset. Place the sewn small heart side 4 pairs into position in the small heart octopus.

- Repeat the above step for the large heart inner side 4 and outer side 4 pieces. Place the sewn large heart side 4 pairs into position in the large heart octopus.

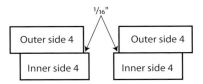

Offset outer side 4 by ⅟₁₆" over inner side 4.

- Beginning with the small heart, pair an inner side 1 with an outer side 1, centering the outer side 1 over the inner side 1 as shown below. Sew them with right sides together. Center and sew the other side 1 pair. Place the sewn side 1 pairs into position in the small heart octopus. Repeat to pair and sew the small heart inner and outer sides 2 and small heart inner and outer sides 3 pieces. Note that the small heart inner side 2 and outer side 2 will be the same length.

- Repeat the above step for the large heart inner and outer sides 1, 2, and 3 pieces. Place the sewn side 1 pairs into position in the large heart octopus.

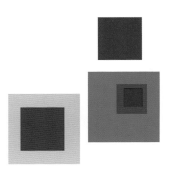

| Outer sides 1 and 3 | Outer side 2 |
| Inner sides 1 and 3 | Inner side 2 |

Position the outer sides over the inner sides for sides 1, 2, and 3.

- Beginning with the small heart, sew the 2 small heart inner side 1 pairs to adjoining sides of the small heart inner square heart base as shown below. Repeat this step for the large heart.

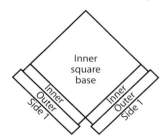

Sew the 2 inner side 1 pairs to adjoining sides of the inner square base.

- Beginning with the small heart, sew the inner side 2, 3, and 4 pairs to the short sides of the inner trapezoid bases as shown below. The 2 trapezoid bases are mirror images of each other. Make sure the side 4 pairs are positioned next to each other when the trapezoid bases are dry-fitted with the square base. Repeat this step for the large heart.

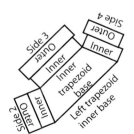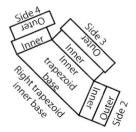

Sew the inner sides 2, 3, and 4 to the inner trapezoid bases.

- Beginning with the small heart, sew the 2 inner trapezoid bases to the inner square base. Repeat this step for the large heart.

- Beginning with the small heart, sew the 2 outer trapezoid bases to the outer square base. Repeat this step for the large heart. Set aside these outer bases.

- Whipstitch the long inner side seams together between the side 4 pairs and then whipstitch the remaining long inner side seams of the small heart; then repeat this step for the large heart.

- Refer to page 16 for information on sewing the lip created by the joining of the outer sides and the inner sides.

- Turn the small heart container right-side out by folding the outer sides down over the inner sides with wrong sides together. Be sure all corners and seams are fully turned and aligned. Repeat this step for the large heart.

- Turn the small heart container upside down and lay the small heart outer base on top of the small heart inner base with wrong sides together. Repeat this step for the large heart.

- Align one edge of the small heart outer base with one edge of a small heart outer side. Use a ladder stitch or whipstitch to attach the outer base to each outer side edge. Repeat this step for the large heart.

- Backstitch to reinforce the outer base stitches at each corner on the small and large hearts. Knot and bury thread.

- Press the top edges of the containers, if needed. Add embellishments or a heart-shaped glass insert in the small heart, if desired.

- Turn the large heart container upside down, place it over the small heart, and enjoy your adorable new box.

Three Nested Hearts

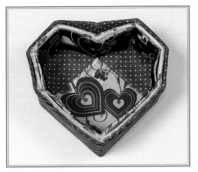

Three heart containers nested together

Make a set of 3 nested hearts using the instructions and the templates for the large heart and the small heart on pages 81–93 and the templates for an extra-large heart on pages 94–99. For additional construction detail, see the general directions on pages 9–16.

Three heart containers shown individually

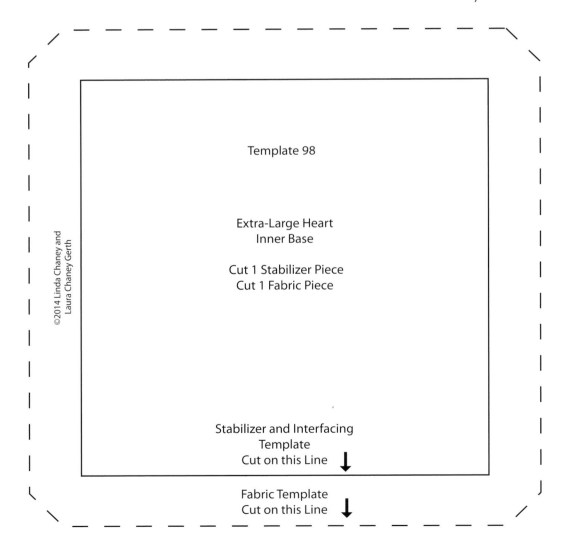

Template 98

Extra-Large Heart
Inner Base

Cut 1 Stabilizer Piece
Cut 1 Fabric Piece

©2014 Linda Chaney and Laura Chaney Gerth

Stabilizer and Interfacing
Template
Cut on this Line ↓

Fabric Template
Cut on this Line ↓

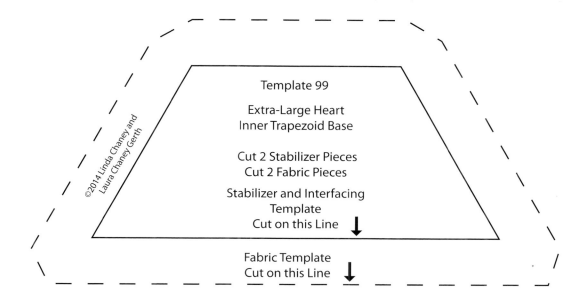

Template 99

Extra-Large Heart
Inner Trapezoid Base

Cut 2 Stabilizer Pieces
Cut 2 Fabric Pieces

Stabilizer and Interfacing
Template
Cut on this Line ↓

Fabric Template
Cut on this Line ↓

©2014 Linda Chaney and
Laura Chaney Gerth

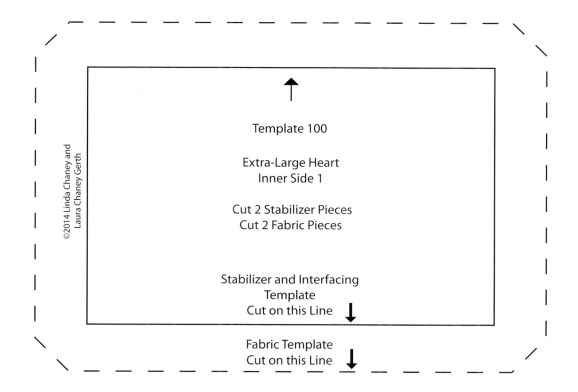

Template 100

Extra-Large Heart
Inner Side 1

Cut 2 Stabilizer Pieces
Cut 2 Fabric Pieces

Stabilizer and Interfacing
Template
Cut on this Line ↓

Fabric Template
Cut on this Line ↓

©2014 Linda Chaney and
Laura Chaney Gerth

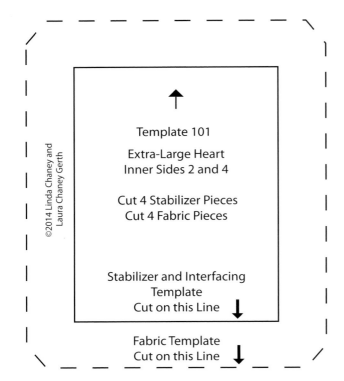

©2014 Linda Chaney and Laura Chaney Gerth

Template 101

Extra-Large Heart
Inner Sides 2 and 4

Cut 4 Stabilizer Pieces
Cut 4 Fabric Pieces

Stabilizer and Interfacing
Template
Cut on this Line

Fabric Template
Cut on this Line

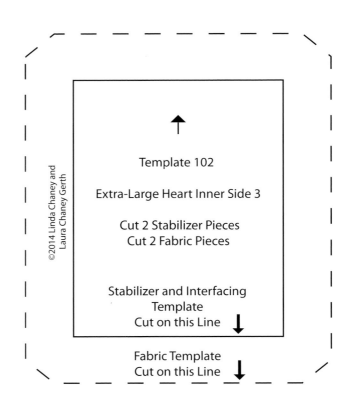

©2014 Linda Chaney and Laura Chaney Gerth

Template 102

Extra-Large Heart Inner Side 3

Cut 2 Stabilizer Pieces
Cut 2 Fabric Pieces

Stabilizer and Interfacing
Template
Cut on this Line

Fabric Template
Cut on this Line

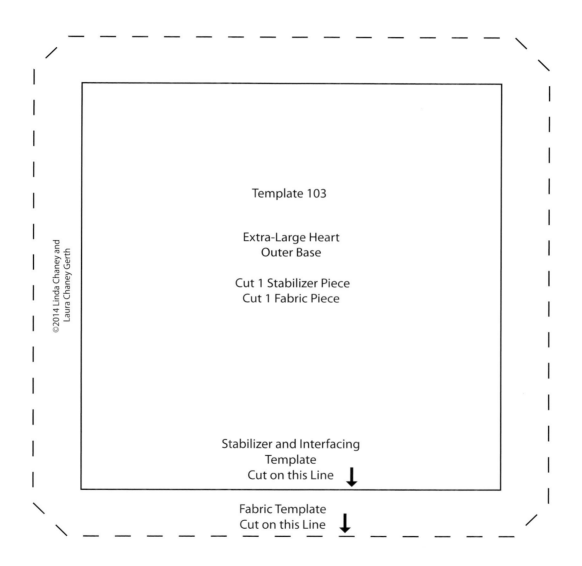

©2014 Linda Chaney and
Laura Chaney Gerth

Template 103

Extra-Large Heart
Outer Base

Cut 1 Stabilizer Piece
Cut 1 Fabric Piece

Stabilizer and Interfacing
Template
Cut on this Line

Fabric Template
Cut on this Line

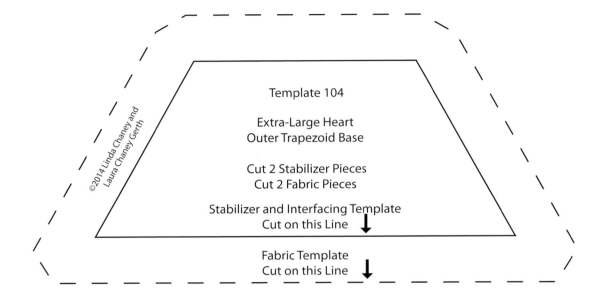

Template 104

Extra-Large Heart
Outer Trapezoid Base

Cut 2 Stabilizer Pieces
Cut 2 Fabric Pieces

Stabilizer and Interfacing Template
Cut on this Line ⬇

Fabric Template
Cut on this Line ⬇

©2014 Linda Chaney and
Laura Chaney Gerth

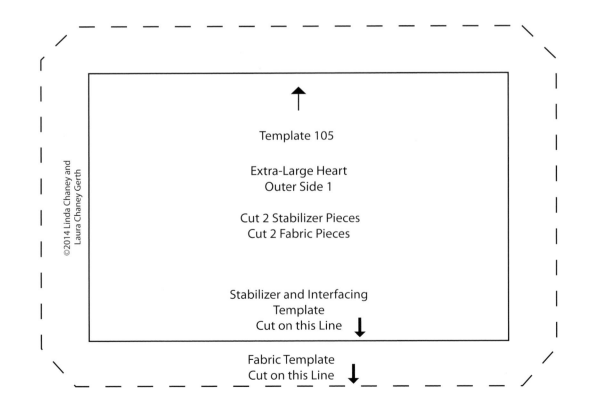

Template 105

Extra-Large Heart
Outer Side 1

Cut 2 Stabilizer Pieces
Cut 2 Fabric Pieces

Stabilizer and Interfacing
Template
Cut on this Line ⬇

Fabric Template
Cut on this Line ⬇

©2014 Linda Chaney and
Laura Chaney Gerth

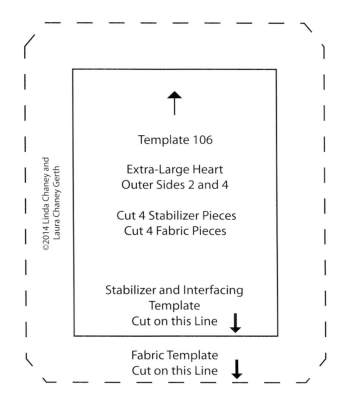

Template 106

Extra-Large Heart
Outer Sides 2 and 4

Cut 4 Stabilizer Pieces
Cut 4 Fabric Pieces

Stabilizer and Interfacing
Template
Cut on this Line ↓

Fabric Template
Cut on this Line ↓

©2014 Linda Chaney and
Laura Chaney Gerth

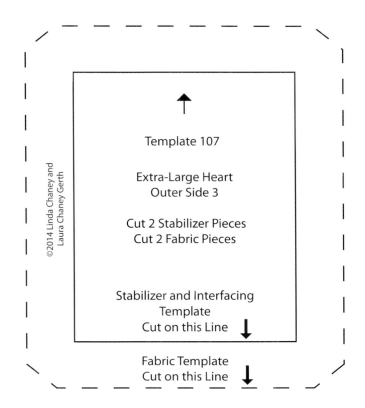

Template 107

Extra-Large Heart
Outer Side 3

Cut 2 Stabilizer Pieces
Cut 2 Fabric Pieces

Stabilizer and Interfacing
Template
Cut on this Line ↓

Fabric Template
Cut on this Line ↓

©2014 Linda Chaney and
Laura Chaney Gerth

A Gallery of Heart-Shaped Containers

The Star Container

A star-shaped container is really exciting to make and use, but it is also quite challenging. Even if you bought this book just to make a star container, please don't start with this project! It really is worth your time to make a cube first and understand the technique before making a star with so many different small pieces and angles.

Pentagonal Star Box

The Pentagonal Star Box has a traditional five-point-star shape with a pieced base. To make a box, you will need to make two stars—a small one for the bottom of the box and a large one for the top. You may also use the two stars as separate containers. Make each section of the star with a different coordinating color or print for a scrappy star or make all of them from the same fabric for a more subdued look.

Materials

Approximately 1 yard of assorted coordinating fabrics and/or scraps makes both stars.

Stabilizer—20" x 23"

¼" fusible tape

Lightweight fusible interfacing (optional)

Assembly

- The steps are summarized below but refer to the general directions for more detail.

- Trace the stabilizer and fabric templates for the inner base and the outer base of the small star onto template material. Repeat using the templates for the inner base and outer base for the large star. Label each template with the information shown on the template and cut them out.

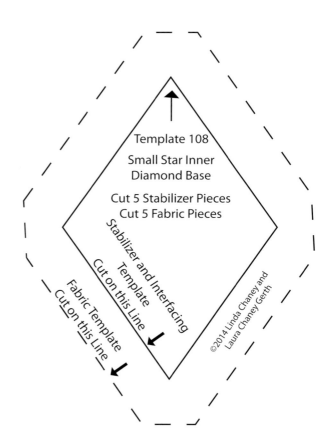

Template 108

Small Star Inner Diamond Base

Cut 5 Stabilizer Pieces
Cut 5 Fabric Pieces

Stabilizer and Interfacing Template
Cut on this Line

Fabric Template
Cut on this Line

©2014 Linda Chaney and Laura Chaney Gerth

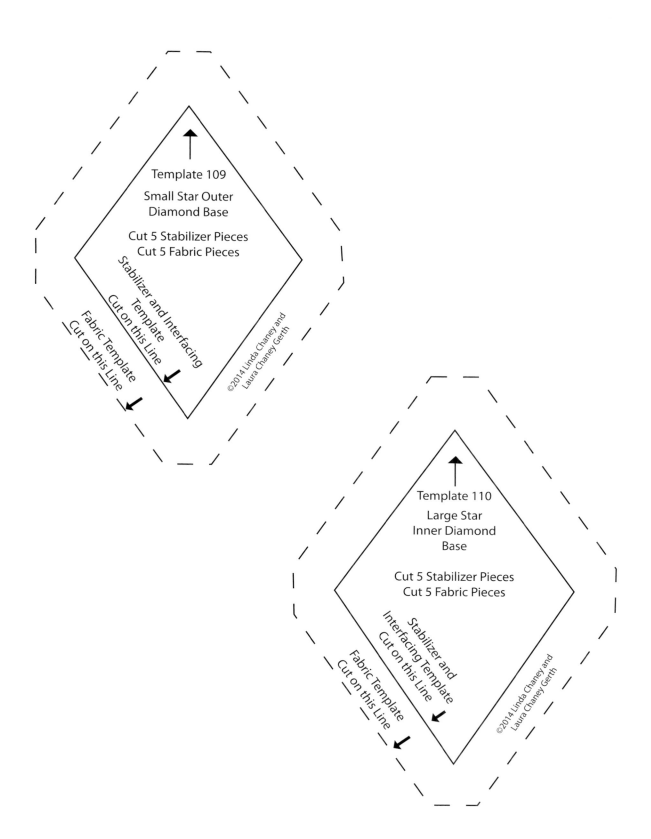

Template 109

Small Star Outer
Diamond Base

Cut 5 Stabilizer Pieces
Cut 5 Fabric Pieces

Stabilizer and Interfacing
Template
Cut on this Line

Fabric Template
Cut on this Line

©2014 Linda Chaney and
Laura Chaney Gerth

Template 110

Large Star
Inner Diamond
Base

Cut 5 Stabilizer Pieces
Cut 5 Fabric Pieces

Stabilizer and
Interfacing Template
Cut on this Line

Fabric Template
Cut on this Line

©2014 Linda Chaney and
Laura Chaney Gerth

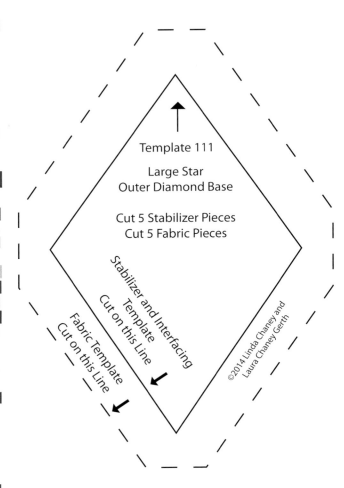

Template 111

Large Star
Outer Diamond Base

Cut 5 Stabilizer Pieces
Cut 5 Fabric Pieces

Stabilizer and Interfacing
Template
Cut on this Line

Fabric Template
Cut on this Line

©2014 Linda Chaney and
Laura Chaney Gerth

- Using the inner base fabric templates and the outer base fabric templates for the small star and the large star, cut 5 fabric pieces from each template. Be sure to label each piece with the information on the template to avoid confusion.

- Using the inner base stabilizer templates and outer base stabilizer templates for the small star and the large star, cut 5 stabilizer pieces from each template. Be sure to label each piece with the information on the template to avoid confusion.

- Trace the stabilizer and fabric templates below for the inner and outer sides of the small star and the inner and outer sides of the large star onto template material. Label each template with the information shown on the template pattern and cut them out.

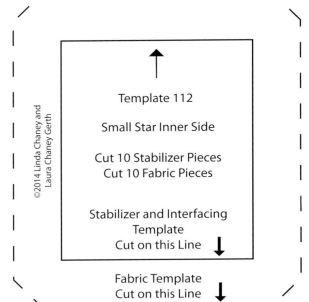

Template 112

Small Star Inner Side

Cut 10 Stabilizer Pieces
Cut 10 Fabric Pieces

Stabilizer and Interfacing
Template
Cut on this Line

Fabric Template
Cut on this Line

©2014 Linda Chaney and
Laura Chaney Gerth

LESSONS FROM LAURA

There is only a slight difference between the sizes of the small star and the large star but the difference is important—it allows the large star to fit over the small one to create a box. Keep the large star pieces separate from the small star pieces to help ensure correct construction.

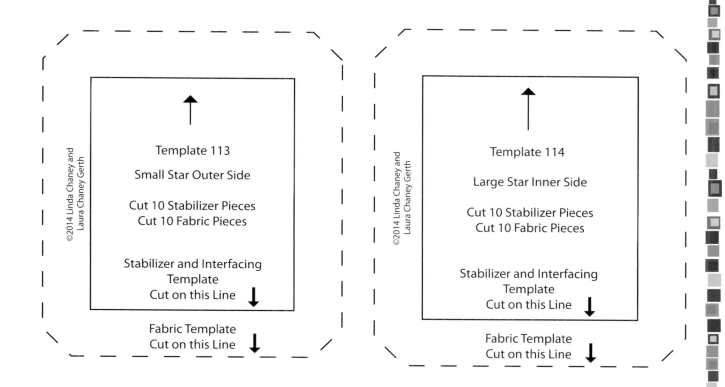

©2014 Linda Chaney and Laura Chaney Gerth

Template 113

Small Star Outer Side

Cut 10 Stabilizer Pieces
Cut 10 Fabric Pieces

Stabilizer and Interfacing Template
Cut on this Line ↓

Fabric Template
Cut on this Line ↓

©2014 Linda Chaney and Laura Chaney Gerth

Template 114

Large Star Inner Side

Cut 10 Stabilizer Pieces
Cut 10 Fabric Pieces

Stabilizer and Interfacing Template
Cut on this Line ↓

Fabric Template
Cut on this Line ↓

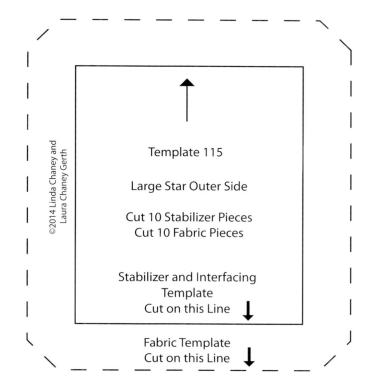

©2014 Linda Chaney and Laura Chaney Gerth

Template 115

Large Star Outer Side

Cut 10 Stabilizer Pieces
Cut 10 Fabric Pieces

Stabilizer and Interfacing Template
Cut on this Line ↓

Fabric Template
Cut on this Line ↓

- Cut 10 fabric pieces from the inner side fabric template and 10 fabric pieces from the outer side fabric template for the small star. Repeat this step for the large star. This will create 40 side fabric pieces—20 for the small star and 20 for the large star. Be sure to label each piece with the information on the template, including arrows, to avoid confusion.

- Cut 10 stabilizer pieces from the inner side stabilizer template and 10 stabilizer pieces from the outer side stabilizer template for the small star. Repeat this step for the large star. This will create 40 side stabilizer pieces—20 for the small star and 20 for the large star. Be sure to label each piece with the information on the template, including arrows, to avoid confusion.

- If embellishing the large star with embroidery, beads, or buttons, use the large star inner and outer base stabilizer templates and the large star outer side stabilizer templates or the outer side strip-cut measurements to cut a piece of interfacing for the bases or sides you want to embellish. Center the interfacing, fusible-side down on the wrong side of the fabric, leaving ½" of fabric uncovered on all sides, and then fuse.

- If embellishing the small star, use the small star inner and outer base stabilizer templates and the small star inner side stabilizer templates to cut a piece of interfacing for the bases or sides you want to embellish. The outer base of the small star is a good place to sign your work so consider applying interfacing to this surface. Center the interfacing, fusible-side down on the wrong side of the fabric, leaving ½" of fabric uncovered on all sides, and then fuse.

Construction
- Pair each fabric piece with its corresponding stabilizer piece.

- Fuse one pair at a time until all of the stabilizer and fabric units are fused.

- Center a stabilizer piece on the wrong side of a fabric piece leaving ½" of fabric uncovered on all sides.

- Apply ¼" fusible tape to one edge of a stabilizer piece. Refer to page 11 for the order in which to apply the tape.

- Fold a fabric edge over the fusible tape and the stabilizer and fuse it to the tape one side at a time. Make sure that the folded fabric completely covers the fusible tape to prevent the gumming of the iron. Be careful not to stretch the bias-cut edges.

- Quilt the large star outer sides or outer base with decorative stitches, if desired.

- Lay out the octopus for the small star right-side up and then lay out the octopus for the large star right-side up.

- Arrange the small star inner bases right-sides up. Sew together the edges shown in red in the diagram below. Be sure all of the arrows are pointing toward the center of the star. Once sewn, the base will not be flat but will bow slightly. Repeat for the large star inner bases.

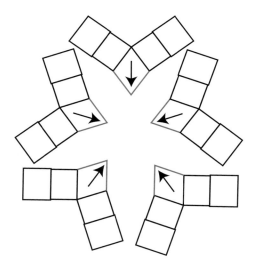

The Pentagonal Star Box octopus

- Arrange the small star outer bases wrong-side up on top of the small star inner bases. Right sides will be together. Be aware how inner bases and outer bases "pair," especially if using different fabrics for different base segments. Repeat for the large star outer bases.

- Sew the small star outer base pieces together where they join in the center. Repeat for the large star outer bases.

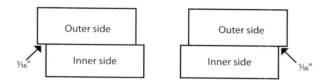

Offset the outer sides and the inner sides of each paired set of sides. Make 5 sets.

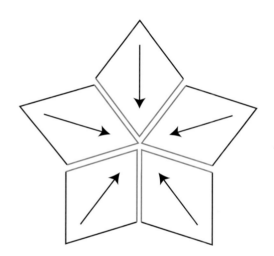

The Star base layout

- Between each point of the stars are 2 inner side pieces and 2 outer side pieces. Pair an outer side with an inner side, offsetting the outer side about 1/16" from the edge of the inner side. Be careful to keep the small star pieces separate from the large star pieces. Refer to the diagram below.

- Sew the small star offset outer side and inner side together. Pair the other outer side with the other inner side, offsetting the outer side about 1/16" from the edge of the inner side in the opposite direction from the first pair. Make 5 of these paired sets. Repeat this step for the large star.

- Lay out the small star paired sets of sides around the points of the inner star base as shown below. Repeat for the large star.

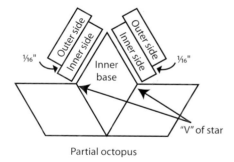

Partial octopus

Position of the paired sets of sides on a diamond point

- Sew the small star inner sides to the inner base, being sure to place the offset edge of the inner side toward the "V" of the star. The overhanging edges of the outer sides will point toward the point of the star. Repeat this step for the large star.

- Whipstitch the small star long side seams together along the "V" first and then those along the points of the stars. Refer to page 16 for information on sewing the lip created by the joining of the outer sides and the inner sides. Repeat for the large star.

- For the large star and the small star, fold the outer sides down over inner sides with wrong sides together.

- Align the outer bases with the inner bases and whipstitch them together.

- Press the top edges of the star containers.

- If using a star-shaped glass bowl, place it in the small star. Turn the large star over and cover the small star.

- Admire your completed Pentagonal Star Box!

Short Pentagonal Star Box

Create a star box with shorter sides using the instructions for the Pentagonal Star on pages 102–108 and Templates 108–111 for the base on pages 102–104. For the short sides, use Templates 116–119. Make sure to use the small bases with the small short sides and the large bases with the large short sides. This little container makes a great gift box for small items. Used separately, it makes two very nice small star-shaped trays to neatly organize a dresser or vanity top. For additional construction information, refer to the general instructions on pages 9–16.

LESSONS FROM LAURA

A star-shaped glass bowl can often be found at your local dollar store to insert into the star box to serve mints or small cookies. The bowl will help keep the inside of the box clean and support its contents.

 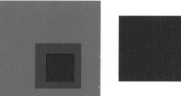

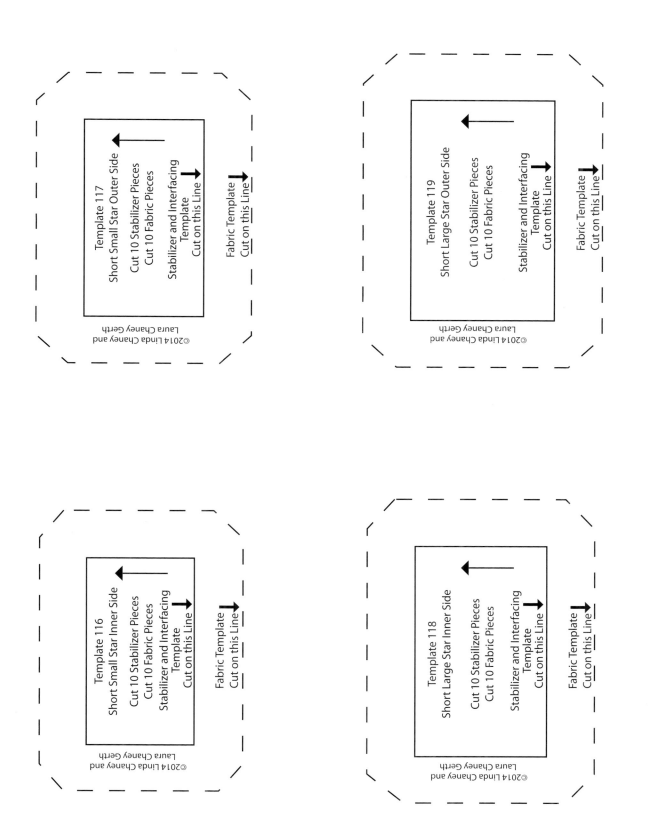

Template 117
Short Small Star Outer Side

Cut 10 Stabilizer Pieces
Cut 10 Fabric Pieces
Stabilizer and Interfacing
Template
Cut on this Line

Fabric Template
Cut on this Line

©2014 Linda Chaney and
Laura Chaney Gerth

Template 119
Short Large Star Outer Side

Cut 10 Stabilizer Pieces
Cut 10 Fabric Pieces
Stabilizer and Interfacing
Template
Cut on this Line

Fabric Template
Cut on this Line

©2014 Linda Chaney and
Laura Chaney Gerth

Template 116
Short Small Star Inner Side

Cut 10 Stabilizer Pieces
Cut 10 Fabric Pieces
Stabilizer and Interfacing
Template
Cut on this Line

Fabric Template
Cut on this Line

©2014 Linda Chaney and
Laura Chaney Gerth

Template 118
Short Large Star Inner Side

Cut 10 Stabilizer Pieces
Cut 10 Fabric Pieces
Stabilizer and Interfacing
Template
Cut on this Line

Fabric Template
Cut on this Line

©2014 Linda Chaney and
Laura Chaney Gerth

A Gallery of Star-Shaped Containers

Chaney and Gerth ▪■▪ Contain It!

ABOUT THE AUTHORS

 Linda Chaney - Mother

A retired research scientist, Linda has sewn since childhood. She grew up making her own clothing and was introduced to the art of quilting by her mother-in-law in 1986. Linda loves learning new techniques, playing with new gadgets, and experimenting with fabric. An avid collector of fabric, she enjoys the opportunity to sew, quilt, and create with her daughter, Laura. Her favorite aspect of creating fabric bowls and vases is drafting new patterns and experimenting with different techniques to achieve her desired result. Her best ideas come in the middle of the night and she can frequently be found in her sewing room at 4 a.m. when genius has struck. Linda lives in Omaha, Nebraska, with her husband who is also a research scientist and supports her quilting addiction.

 Laura Chaney Gerth - Daughter

Laura works in higher education with international students and scholars coming to study or conduct research in the United States. Although she dabbled in sewing and quilting during her childhood, she didn't begin creating in earnest until her sophomore year of college. Her first true project was inspired by a visit to her grandmother's quilter in Amish country. Under the tutelage of both her grandmother and mother, Laura completed her first small wallhanging and began looking to the next challenge. She loves the opportunity to quilt and create with her mother and looks forward to their annual mother-daughter trip to AQS QuiltWeek® in Paducah, Kentucky, each year. Laura lives in San Francisco, California, with her two cats who love to help her sew and quilt.

Linda Chaney and Laura Chaney Gerth can be contacted at their blog: www.prairiesewnstudios.com.

More AQS Books

This is only a small selection of the books available from the American Quilter's Society. AQS books are known worldwide for timely topics, clear writing, beautiful color photos, and accurate illustrations and patterns. The following books are available from your local bookseller, quilt shop, or public library.

#8532

#8353

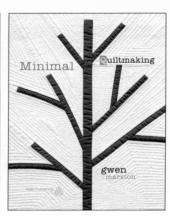
#1423

Minimal Quiltmaking
gwen marston
#1546

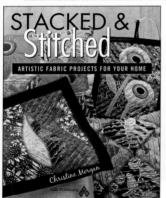
#8767

#1417

#8764

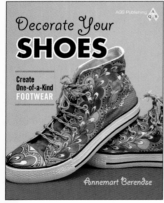
#8766

#8661

LOOK for these books nationally.
CALL or **VISIT** our website at
www.AmericanQuilter.com
1-800-626-5420